T0025589

HERO
for the
HUNGRY

THE LIFE & WORK *of* NORMAN BORLAUG

FEEDING MINDS
PRESS

Text © 2022 Peggy Thomas

Illustrations © 2022 Sam Kalda

ISBN 9781948898096

Library of Congress Control Number: 2021952313

Published by Feeding Minds Press, Washington, D.C.
All rights reserved. No part of this book may be reproduced or
transmitted in any form or by any means, electronic or mechanical,
including photocopying, recording, or by any information storage and
retrieval system without permission in writing from the publisher.
For permissions contact info@feedingmindspress.com

Our books can be purchased in bulk for educational purposes.
Please contact your local bookseller or Feeding Minds Press at
info@feedingmindspress.com

Designed by Michele Sheedy
Art Direction by Mary Burns
Edited by Emma D. Dryden

Printed in the United States of America
First Edition
10 9 8 7 6 5 4 3 2 1

HERO
for the
HUNGRY
THE LIFE & WORK of NORMAN BORLAUG

by

PEGGY THOMAS

illustrated by

SAM KALDA

Dedications

For all those dedicated to ending world hunger.

~ P.T.

To the farmers and gardeners in my family,
past and present.

~ S.K.

Acknowledgments

I'd like to thank Tom Spindler at the Norman Borlaug Heritage Foundation for aiding in my research; Keegan Kautzky, the World Food Prize Senior Director of Global Youth Programs and Partnerships for sharing stories of his time with Norm; and special thanks to Jeanie Borlaug Laube for adding her blessings to this project and for carrying on her father's work in food security as chair of the Borlaug Global Rust Initiative, and creating the Jeanie Borlaug Laube Women in Triticum Early Career Award which celebrates and supports women in wheat research. Thank you to everyone at Feeding Minds Press; to editor Emma Dryden; copy editor Karen Galle at Hilltop Editorial Services; Sam Kalda for bringing Norm to life in his lovely illustrations; and especially to Julia Recko, AFBFA Education Outreach Director, for her infectious enthusiasm. It's a pleasure working with all of you.

~ P.T.

Table of Contents

PROLOGUE

OCTOBER 20, 1970

Norman Borlaug stands in a golden sea of thigh-high wheat. He's the man in the middle of a small group of men, their heads bent to hear every word their teacher says. Out of the corner of his eye, Norm notices a cloud of dust rise up in the distance and move along the road on the other side of an irrigation ditch. Someone's coming. As the car approaches, Norm continues to instruct his students—two from Romania, two from Mexico, one from Brazil, and another from the United States. All of them are sweat-stained and dirty under the hot Mexican sun.

The car stops. Norm's wife Margaret steps out. Alarm bells go off in Norm's head. Margaret looks flustered, which isn't like her at all.

Norm hurries down the row to the edge of the ditch. "What's wrong?" he calls out. Has one of the children been in an accident? Is his mother or father sick?

It has to be something urgent for Margaret to drive all the way out here from Mexico City.

Margaret shakes her head and hollers, "Norman, you've won the Nobel Peace Prize."

Now it's Norm's turn to shake his head. "No. No," he says calmly. "That can't be, Margaret. Someone's pulling your leg." He waves Margaret off, then turns back to his wheat-breeding students. Why on earth would anyone give *him* the Nobel Peace Prize?[1]

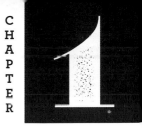
I-O-WAY

"Food is the moral right of all who are born into this world."[2]

A young Norm stood in a muddy field on a farm in the northeast corner of Iowa. He hoisted a rock and tossed it onto the sled just like his grandad did. Why do we have to pick up rocks in the field EVERY year? It was his umpteenth question of the day. But Grandad Nels, Norm's favorite person in the world, didn't mind.

"Never stop asking why things are the way they are," Grandad Nels told him.

One day, Norm asked, "Why can't I stay home from school?" Sitting in a stuffy one-room schoolhouse wasn't nearly as exciting as fishing in the creek or listening to Grandad Nels tell stories of the old country. Norm liked hearing about how his great-grandparents fled Norway to settle in Saude, Iowa, and how they'd lived in the small log cabin that now slumped out back, acting as a toolshed.

Grandad Nels tapped his grandson's blonde noggin. "Norm-boy," he said in his light Norwegian accent, "it's better to fill your mind now if you want to fill your belly later."

So, Norm hurried off to school to fill his mind.

Blizzard

Norm was six years old in 1920 when he entered New Oregon Township School #8 for the first time. Kids from miles around had been attending this one-room schoolhouse since Grandad Nels was little. Norm even spotted his dad's initials carved into one of the desktops. Norm traced the jaggedy *H.B.* under his fingers. It felt good knowing his father and grandfather had walked the very same route, sat at the very same desks, and learned the very same lessons. "If they could do it, I could too."

That first winter was particularly brutal. During lessons, the room grew dark. The teacher, Miss Halvorson, lit the oil lamps, but Norm still had trouble seeing the figures on his slate. Outside, a solid wall of snow blasted across the open fields. Wind howled and the schoolhouse creaked as icy chills slipped through the cracks. Miss Halvorson announced school was ending early.

One of the older students helped little Norm bundle up, and led him and the others home. As the smallest child in the group, Norm fell in to the middle of the single file line. His twelve-year-old cousin Sina brought up the rear.

As they trudged through drifts, the wind whipped Norm's breath

Picking Rocks

In the winter, frost pushes rock up through the soil to the surface. In the spring, farmers (and their kids) walk the field picking up rocks that could damage their machines. In areas like northeastern Iowa the rocks can be large. They were left behind by retreating glaciers thousands of years ago.

away and sliced at his face. He tried to practice something else Grandad had told him—don't be afraid.

The melting snow inside his boots numbed his feet, making him stumble. Totally exhausted from trying to keep up, Norm collapsed in a snowbank. He wanted nothing more than to stay there and sleep.

Someone ripped Norm's scarf away from his face and jerked his head up. "Get up! Get up!" Cousin Sina yelled. All the other kids huddled miserably against the wind while Norm just lay there. They were exhausted too. The oldest boy yanked Norm to his feet. Sina took Norm's hand and dragged him, tired, cold, and embarrassed, all the way home.

The moment Norm stumbled into the kitchen he burst into tears. As little as he was, Norm knew he'd let everyone down; by stopping in

the storm, he'd put all the other kids' lives at risk. He never wanted to be that thoughtless again.

Norm's mother peeled off each wet layer of clothing and sat him by the stove. His grandmother Emma cut him a thick slice of bread, still warm from the oven. Many years later Norm said that no food tasted sweeter than the bread Grandmother baked the day he nearly died.

Filling the Mind

Each morning Miss Halvorson gave Norm his daily instructions. She checked his progress by having him recite lessons aloud. "We read aloud, spelled aloud, and sung out grammar drills and multiplication tables at our little voice-box's highest volume setting." One of Norm's favorite first lessons was memorizing the Iowa Corn Song:

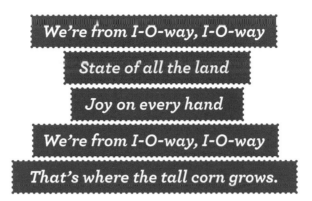

We're from I-O-way, I-O-way

State of all the land

Joy on every hand

We're from I-O-way, I-O-way

That's where the tall corn grows.

While they sang, Norm would look around at his classmates. There were Norwegians, Czechoslovakians, Germans ... kids from all different backgrounds, different traditions, singing with different accents. But Norm realized those differences were artificial; they didn't matter. Inside, all the children had the same wants and needs. They were all just American farm kids in school.

Filling the Belly

When Norm wasn't at school, he was an integral part of the Borlaug belly-filling process. As soon as his toddle turned into a trot, his father had him stacking wood, picking rocks, and collecting chicken eggs. With every inch he grew, his parents tacked on another chore. The job Norm hated the most was weeding. As soon as he finished, he'd turn around to see new weeds popping up to taunt him. But Norm never complained. No one did. If you wanted to eat, you had to work. There were no convenience stores on the corner, no microwave ovens, no pre-cooked, pre-packaged foods.

Most of what the Borlaugs needed they found or grew on their 120 acres. Like a living machine, everything on the farm had a purpose. The horses powered the plow, thresher, and buggy. Dairy cows provided milk, and cream for butter. Fields of clover supplied a pasture for grazing, and acres of corn and oats fattened the hogs and steer.

No matter how well Dad and Grandad planned, they were always at the mercy of Mother Nature. Insect damage, crop disease, late frost, early frost, too much rain, or no rain at all could mean empty stomachs in the winter. Hunger lingered, threatening, like a distant storm cloud on the horizon, but not the stomach-rumbling kind of hunger. This was hunger with a capital H. The kind of Hunger that makes a child cry, stunts their growth, and dulls the mind. The kind of Hunger that chased Norm's great-grandparents out of Norway.

The Borlaugs never let anyone go hungry. If a neighbor fell on hard times or became ill, Norm helped his mother deliver soup to them, even if a family was quarantined with the deadly flu. Norm would leave the pot of soup on the steps, wave to the fevered children through the window, and collect the empty pot the following day.

Norm's family was luckier than most. There were only a few times when the family went without. Once, when Norm was too small to remember, a disease destroyed their wheat crop and most of the wheat in the Midwest. Norm knew about it only because Grandad Nels still occasionally grumbled about the year there was no "proper bread" on the dinner table.

Fleeing Famine

Norm's great-grandparents, Ole and Solveig Borlaug, were farmers in Norway. They were like millions of other farmers across Europe who experienced the horror of walking out to their fields on a fall day to find their potato vines wilted and black. A foul odor hung in the air. Hurriedly they dug up their crop hoping to find a few healthy potatoes, but the spuds turned to mush in their hands. The odor of decay grew stronger. Their plants had been attacked by a fungus called potato blight.

The fungus had been lurking in the soil through the hot summer until autumn conditions made the soil warm and wet. Then the fungus released billions of spores in the air. Carried by the wind, the fungus spread. In the 1840's the potato blight floated west to Ireland, then north to Norway.

Like many others faced with starvation, Ole and Solveig left their farm and sailed to America. They settled in Iowa among family and friends, built a small log cabin, and created a farm on County Road in the village of Saude.

If Norm's great-grandparents had stayed in Norway, they may have been among the 50,000 Norwegians who died of Hunger and disease.

Home of Their Own

By the time Norm was eight years old, he had a six-year-old sister Palma and a three-year-old sister Charlotte. The Borlaug house was overflowing. After much discussion, Norm's parents used their life savings to buy land next to Grandad's. They built a home—Modern Home #209—purchased from the 1922 Sears, Roebuck & Co. catalogue. It cost $981.00.

The square, two-story home offered plenty of space for everyone. "For the first time my parents, my sisters, and I were together and by ourselves. Our circle was complete; the world seemed right." He didn't even miss Grandad, because with a combined farm, they were all up at dawn with chores to do. Humming a tune, Norm lit the stove, fed the chickens, and hand-cranked the machine that separated cream from the milk. After a hearty egg breakfast, Norm and his sisters walked to the schoolhouse. In the afternoons, Norm chopped and stacked wood, hauled hay, brushed the horses, and trimmed the wicks on the oil lamps.

In the evenings the only sounds were natural ones: lilting Norwegian conversation, hymn singing, a low bellow from a cow in the field, wind rustling through a sea of corn. On clear nights, Norm grabbed blankets and he and his sisters would snuggle on the porch, listening for the whistle of the Milwaukee train pulling into the distant town of Cresco. Norm remembered, "It was the only time we sensed we were part of a wider sphere."

Tucked under those blankets, Norm could never have imagined how wide his world would get, and it would start with a visit from his cousin Sina.

SPARTAN DAYS

"Whatever I have become, these people [of Cresco] are a part of it. They taught me to give the best that is within me."[12]

Sina had become the new teacher at School #8, and Norm was her student. Near the end of Norm's eighth year, she stopped by the Borlaug's home to discuss Norm's future. He should go to high school, she said. Norm's mother and father agreed.

Most boys in their early teens quit school to work on the family farm. But Grandad Nels had always encouraged everyone in the family to get an education. He said it was the only protection you could count on when times got tough.

"As a scholar, he's no great shakes," Sina said of Norm, "but he's got grit."[13]

Sending Norm to school would mean losing a farmhand, so his father took advantage of Norm's muscles while he could. The Borlaugs had taken out what little money they had in the bank and invested in material for a barn. Throughout the summer Norm sawed and hammered until the new barn stood tall against a sea of corn.

On the first day of high school Norm's tanned arms flexed with a carpenter's muscles. He eyed the three-story school building in front of him before joining the rush of more than three hundred students inside. If Norm worried about making friends in ninth grade, he never let on. His kind smile, blue eyes, and tousled blonde hair caught the girls' attention, while the boys gravitated to Norm's easygoing energy and spunk.

He participated in nearly every club and activity, eager to learn as much as he could. He sang bass in glee club, became stage manager for the operetta, and participated in the agricultural club. His excitement, however, made him unaware of the growing unease that lurked throughout the entire country.

Crash!

In October 1929, the stock market crashed. Stocks being traded on the New York Stock Exchange lost fifty percent of their value. Prices continued to drop, and the fallout swept across the nation like a tidal wave. Businesses closed. People lost their jobs. Families couldn't afford to buy food. Farmers couldn't pay their mortgages.

Norm knew that the Borlaug's money was safely sheltered in lumber, nails, and roofing shingles, but he couldn't help thinking about all the farmers who weren't so lucky. Many had to abandon their farms. Able-bodied boys dropped out of high school to support their families. But not Norm. The Borlaugs kept Norm in school.

Feeding the Soil

Besides his regular courses of English, math, and history, Norm also took classes in agriculture. Norm might have thought he knew all he needed to know about farming by watching his father and grandad, but he soon discovered that the agricultural teacher, Mr. Harry Schroder, had a few surprises to share. Schroder was fresh from Iowa State College, one of the first agricultural colleges in the country. He taught the new science of farm management, soil improvement, and horticulture.

One morning Mr. Schroder surprised the class when he led the students down the road to a farmer's field to do an experiment. Mr. Schroder instructed the class to measure out several small square plots, each one the same size. Then they prepared each plot for planting. The first square was left untouched to serve as the control for the experiment. In all the other squares, Norm and his classmates

FOOD FOR THOUGHT

NPK

Nitrogen (N), phosphorus (P), and potassium (K) are key nutrients plants need to survive. They are commonly found in soil and absorbed by plants through the root system. Each nutrient has a different job to do. Nitrogen fuels plant growth. Phosphorus stimulates root growth and seed production. Potassium helps a plant fight disease. As plants grow and take up the available nutrients, they leave the soil less fertile. To keep plants healthy year after year, farmers must add commercial fertilizer or organic material like compost or manure to the soil.

mixed varying amounts of nitrogen, phosphorus, and potassium into the soil. Then they planted the same amount of corn in each plot.

Throughout the growing season, the boys weeded and recorded the size and vigor of the corn. At harvest, Norm was astonished to find that some of the fertilized plots yielded twice as much corn as the unfertilized control plot, which resembled the crop on his father's farm. The Borlaugs didn't use fertilizer either. At that time, not many farmers did.

Norm could only imagine how life-changing it would have been if his father and grandfather had known about adding fertilizer to soil to increase their crop yield. His father would have had more income. The family would have been able to make improvements like building a home and a new barn much sooner. They would have been able to move from subsistence farming—growing only enough food for themselves—to commercial farming where they also sold food on the market.

The Borlaugs Buy a Tractor

While Norm was learning about the new science and technology available to farmers, Grandad was taking advantage of it. Norm came home one day to find a brand new Fordson Model F tractor sitting in the yard. A whopping twenty-horsepower engine powered the clunky-looking vehicle with studded back wheels. Norm didn't have to feel guilty about not helping out. The tractor effortlessly replaced Norm *and* the draft horses.

A tractor not only saved on man- and horsepower, it saved money, time, and land. Now the acres of land that the Borlaugs used to grow feed for horses and cattle could be planted with a cash crop like sweet corn or potatoes. The tractor didn't need a rubdown or liniment at the end of the day, either.

The Borlaugs sold their work horses and most of their cattle. They breathed easier knowing there was money to pay for a good education for Norm and his sisters. "Country kids like me finally could follow our heart's desire," Norm said, "and that amounted to the ultimate freedom."[14]

Sportsman

All that freedom allowed Norm to participate in sports at Cresco High. He was particularly thrilled to join the football team, which had become the Iowa State Champions thanks to senior and star running back, George Champlin. Unfortunately, Norm didn't get to play with George nor did the Spartans continue their championship streak, but Norm loved the challenge and camaraderie. At 140 pounds he was smaller than most of his teammates, but he was fierce on the line.

When football season was over, Norm threw himself into wrestling. He excelled, thanks to coach David Bartelma.

A former member of the U.S. Olympic wrestling squad, Bartelma was an inspiration to the high-schoolers, and his coaching style resonated with Norm. "Give the best that God gave you," Coach said. "If you don't do that, don't bother to compete."[15]

On the mat, Norm resembled a bulldog on a bone. "Wrestling made me mentally tough," he said.[16] There was no one to blame if he won or lost. It was all up to him. Norm quickly became the star athlete on a winning team. Newspaper headlines bragged, *Matmen Crush Eagle Grove. Grapplers Cop District Title.* In Norm's senior year, the team was undefeated, and he went on to place third in the state.

For the first time, Norm began to sense what he was capable of, and imagined the real possibilities of life away from the farm. Inspired by Mr. Schroder and Coach Bartelma, Norm decided to become a teacher and wrestling coach. However, that meant putting other, less realistic, dreams aside.

A League of His Own

Ever since Grandad brought home their first radio, Norm had been hooked on the Chicago Cubs. When the Cubs played, Norm would dash in from his chores to tune in for the score. "Deep down," he said, "I knew that one day I'd be their second base."[17]

Unfortunately, Cresco High did not have a baseball team. How was he supposed to become a baseball player with no team to play with?

Why not start a baseball league of my own? Norm thought.

In 1929, Norm corralled his friends to play for the town of Saude.

In a cow pasture outside of town, Norm paced out a diamond and laid bases, which were sacks filled with sand. Everyone brought whatever equipment they could scrounge up—bats that splintered hands and gloves nearly worn-through. Occasionally Norm would arrive early at the field, and discover the gift of a new bat or a few new balls left by a generous fan.

Next, Norm went to the nearby towns of Protivin, Jerico, Spillville, and Schley. He urged them to form teams of their own. Soon Norm had a real baseball league, and was figuring out a playing schedule.

Each town baseball team harbored a strong ethnic heritage. Norm's team from Saude was mostly Norwegian. Spillville players were Czech. Others were Irish or German. It didn't matter. All the boys loved all-American baseball.

With little else to entertain folks on a Saturday, the games attracted a crowd. By Norm's senior year, the Saude-Spillville rivalry had become a feature at Spillville's annual Fourth of July festivities. That year, 1932, the sun blazed and the air hung heavy. Even so, more than two hundred people showed up to support their favorite players. Over the years, folks have forgotten the play-by-play and the final score, but Norm never did. Saude lost in extra innings. Still, Norm remembered that day fondly. As the moon rose, fireworks lit the sky over Spillville's Dvorak Riverside Park. Listening to all the different accents around him, Norm marveled at the way people's similarities outweighed their differences.

Graduate Dreams

In May 1932, Norm graduated high school with honors. He earned the Legion Citizenship Award for courage, character, service, and scholarship, and Bartelma awarded him an athletic medal. Even so, there was little to be happy about. Because of the Great Depression, there was no money to send Norm to university as he, his parents, and grandparents had always dreamed.

After graduation Norm hung out with two friends, Erv Upton and Bob Smylie. Norm and Erv were farm kids, but Bob's father was an out-of-work school superintendent. Like so many other families around the country during the Great Depression, the Smylies floundered, moving from town to town looking for work. They had landed in Cresco where the family ran a twenty-four-hour gas station on Highway 9. Bob worked the night shift.

Although the boys were happy to have graduated, there was little else to celebrate. Even so, Bob scribbled lofty predictions in Norm and Erv's yearbooks: Erv, he wrote, would become "Senator Upton in Washington D.C." and Norm would receive the "Congressional Award for Valor."[18]

Only time would tell if Bob's predictions would come true.

Penny Sale

Fifteen miles west of Cresco, in the little town of Saratoga, Norm followed signs to a public foreclosure auction. Some poor family couldn't pay their mortgage, so the bank was auctioning off their home and all of their possessions. Chairs, tables, pots, and pans littered the lawn. Out-of-town shoppers examined the plow, the beds, and the dishes, hoping to find cheap bargains. Norm had heard of "penny sales" like this, but had never witnessed one before.

When the auctioneer struck his gavel, neighbors crowded around the out-of-towners to prevent them from bidding. This was technically illegal, but the sheriff overlooked it. Once the out-of-towners left, the neighbors stepped up to purchase everything for mere pennies. Five cents for a team of horses. Twenty-five cents for all the living room furniture, a few dollars for the house and land. By the end of the auction, the greedy bank made only a

Helping Farmers

Leading into the Great Depression, farmers were producing too much which drove down prices. The Agricultural Adjustment Act (AAA) of 1933 was passed. It set limits on the size of the crops and herds farmers could produce. The farmers that agreed to limit production earned money. Most farmers signed up and soon government checks were flowing into rural mail boxes where the money could help pay bank debts or tax payments.

fraction of what they were owed. The neighbors then gifted the home back to the grateful family and carried all the furniture back into the house.

The family wasn't much better off than they'd been before the penny sale, but thanks to their neighbors their future looked a little brighter. The whole sad experience lingered in Norm's mind: how a community had broken the law to help a family who, through no fault of their own, had fallen on bad times. Norm always considered himself law-abiding, but that day he realized that the *right* thing to do was not always the *lawful* thing to do.

New Hope

In February 1933, Cresco hosted the Midwest Amateur University Wrestling Tournament. Even though he hadn't wrestled for nearly a year, Norm entered the competition. Excited to be back on the mat, Norm breezed through his first bouts.

In the final round he faced the All State College Tournament winner from Iowa State Teacher's College. This boy was in seriously good shape. Norm knew it would take more than nervous energy to take him down.

Point for point, Norm stayed with him in true bulldog style. By the third period the score was tied. The referee called for overtime.

After a short break they were back on the mat circling each other like hungry bears. Norm grabbed, pulled, and had the All State champ on his back. The whistle blew. Norm thought he'd won. But the whistle was not for him. The referee awarded his opponent points for an escape. Norm had lost.

As Norm walked off the mat, the Iowa State coach called him over. Impressed with Norm's skill, the man suggested that Norm apply to Iowa State Teacher's College in the fall. The coach would even help Norm find a job to help pay tuition. It was all the encouragement Norm needed. He applied and was accepted.

The rest of the winter, Norm set traps in the woods to catch weasel, muskrat, and skunk. He sold the pelts to a dealer in Kansas City. Each pelt only earned a dollar or two, but once, he caught a mink that earned him the most money he'd ever earned at one time— ten dollars. In spring and summer he continued working odd jobs including cutting fence posts for thirty-five cents a day. By the end of the summer of 1933, Norm had sixty dollars in his pocket and images of campus life running through his head.

About a week before leaving for Iowa State, George Champlin, the former Cresco star running back, paid Norm a visit. George was now a student at the University of Minnesota and was scouting potential football players for the University's Golden Gophers.

Norm couldn't believe his ears. He'd love to play football again. But he was committed to Iowa State Teacher's College. Besides, Norm said, I don't have the money for a big university education and probably couldn't get in anyway.

George may have been fast on his feet, but he was also a fast talker. He countered all of Norm's excuses. Can't afford it? Champlin could get him a job. Can't get in? Norm hadn't even tried yet. Besides, George was only offering Norm a football tryout. "Drive up with me and see for yourself," George said. "If you don't like it, you can hitchhike home."[19]

George turned to go, then stopped and added, "Erv Upton's going to try out...."

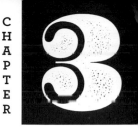
NORM MEETS WORLD

....

"Reach for the stars."[20]

That clinched it. If his friend Erv was going then Norm was too. He was always up for an adventure. Besides, it was just for a few days. He'd have plenty of time to get back to Iowa State before the first day of school.

Maybe Norm really believed that. Or maybe, somewhere deep inside, Norm knew this was the opportunity he'd been dreaming of, because he packed everything he owned, all the money he'd saved, plus the eleven silver dollars Grandad Nels had given him, before the boys drove away the next day.

Minneapolis

Nineteen-year old Norm bounced in the rumble seat and watched Iowa fade away. He'd never been out of the state before. Soon the skyline of Minneapolis appeared. Its only skyscraper, thirty-two stories tall, towered over the city. For the first time, Norm saw

streetcars, sidewalks, and the devastating effects of the Depression. Storefronts were boarded up. Unemployed men were hanging out in parks, and people—even children—were sleeping in doorways.

As George pulled the car up in front of 505 15th Avenue SE, Norm craned his neck to take in the three-story brick building. Erv and Norm followed George up two flights of stairs to a one-room apartment furnished with two beds, a wooden table, and four rickety chairs. To Norm it was perfect.

Next, they had to get a job so they could eat, even if it was just for a few days. Luckily, the local university coffee shop always hired student staff who worked, not for money, but for meals.

The manager, a hulking Olympic hammer thrower, eyed the two farm boys, and with only George's enthusiastic recommendation,

hired Norm and Erv on the spot. "Come back tomorrow morning at seven," the man said. "Work a shift, get a meal."[21]

The promise of breakfast was enough to get Norm and Erv up and out early the next morning. Neither one of them had ever worked in a restaurant before. Between the cook barking at them and questions from the customers, Norm and Erv fumbled their way through the breakfast run. On their break, they gobbled their meal of toast and prunes and gulped coffee before starting the lunch shift. By dinnertime, Norm was still mixing up orders and sloshing coffee. When George arrived to check on their progress, Norm overheard the manager grumble, "Either I'll make a waiter out of Borlaug or I'll kill him."[22]

It could have been the thrill of being in the big city or all the new experiences he encountered, but Norm was confident that Minneapolis was where he was supposed to be. Impulsively, he called Iowa State Teacher's College and said he wasn't coming. Then, he took his school file to the University of Minnesota.

The admissions officer took one look at Norm's course list and said Norm was missing required courses in science and math. Norm would have to take a test to prove he was ready to attend university. Norm hadn't taken a test or used his high school math or science in more than a year, but that didn't stop him from marching into the testing room the next Saturday.

When the test was over, Norm knew he'd "flunked it beautifully."[23]

He wondered, Now what will I do? Norm had recklessly thrown away a sure education at the Teacher's College and now had nothing.

"At that moment I considered myself a complete flop," he said.[24] What would he tell his parents?

He'd have a long time to think about it as he hitchhiked home. But first he had to say goodbye to George.

Fortunately for Norm, George's personality matched his game-playing strategy. He never gave up on anything, including his friends. George marched Norm to the dean's office and asked if Norm could have a second chance. Slapping Norm on the shoulder, George declared, "He's not as dumb as you think."[25]

With that glowing endorsement, the dean enrolled Norm in a new junior college program for promising students who needed extra help before they joined university courses. Finally, Norm was a college student. But would he be a football player?

At the Golden Gophers tryouts, the college players towered over him. Norm took his place on the line and steeled himself for the hard hits. By the end, Norm felt as if he'd been trampled by every horse on the planet. Erv didn't fare any better. Even the ever-optimistic George had to admit Norm and Erv were better off joining the wrestling team, which they did.

Hunger Strikes!

A couple of hours before his evening shift at the coffee shop, Norm took a walk. The fall air refreshed his spirit. He crossed the Washington Avenue Bridge and stopped to watch the Mississippi River flowing below him. On the west side of the river was the

Warehouse District where businesses distributed everything from shoes to shovels. Turning a corner, Norm heard angry voices. He followed the noise to the entrance of one of the warehouses.

Gaunt, desperate men shouted at beefy guards positioned behind a tall steel gate. The guards slapped billy clubs into their palms. Behind the guards, a dozen shiny white milk trucks idled. It was a strike. The shouting men out front were protesting a cut in wages. They only wanted what they'd had before. Unfortunately, the company had hired other men so desperate that they'd work for next to nothing.

Norm watched as the steel gates screeched open.

The armed guards, swinging their clubs, advanced on the strikers.

Unarmed, the protestors panicked. They backed away. Some fell and were trampled by the frightened crowd.

Norm retreated too. Soon he felt the rough brick of a wall at his back. His heart pounded as the mass of angry men pressed in on him. His ears rang from the assault of shouts, cries, and moans.

A guard swung his billy club. Norm heard the sickening *crunch* as the club connected with a skull. Bleeding, the man fell to the ground.

The milk trucks revved their engines. In tight formation they rolled into the street.

An ambulance siren blared its approach.

Shaken and scared, Norm ran, his legs trembling like rubber.

The violence had erupted so quickly. Why? Those men only

"

"I was freed from the crush only after the milk trucks had gone past.... Bodies and blood were scattered and spattered over the street. By then, the company guards were back behind the gates. Again shoulder-to-shoulder, they stood stiff and seemingly unmoved by the sickening sights their own hands had created."[26]

wanted their jobs back. They wanted to feed their families. Hunger with a capital *H* had turned fathers and brothers into an angry mob. "Obviously, peace and prosperity couldn't survive without food," Norm said later. "Even the most serene society could turn violent. What have hungry people to lose?"[27]

HUNGER DAYS

"Without food, all the other things we take for granted—clothing, housing, education, and employment—are of secondary importance."[28]

During a meal break at the coffee shop, Norm read a text book while gobbling his prunes and toast. He looked up to see a young woman watching him. "What are you studying?" she asked. Norm liked her confident smile and the way her black hair curled around her face. She introduced herself as Margaret Gibson, and she'd just been hired as a new server. From that day on, Norm never ate alone. He planned his breaks so he could always sit beside her.

Margaret grew up in Oklahoma and was a couple of years older than Norm. She was studying at the University of Minnesota to be a teacher. Besides waiting tables, she also babysat to earn money for her room and board.

Perhaps Norm wanted to show off for Margaret, or he was just being impulsive again, but after a month of classes in the junior college program, Norm asked the dean for a transfer to the university program. The dean said no.

Norm wouldn't give up. Every few weeks he'd ask again. Finally, the Dean examined Norm's mid-term scores, and after a long pause ... agreed.

"What would you like to major in?" the Dean asked.

Norm declared, "Forestry." It would allow him to be active and out of doors. Plus, forestry majors were in demand.

Hamburger Helper

One chilly morning in 1934, Norm and Margaret arrived at the coffee shop to discover the door locked and a "GONE OUT OF BUSINESS" sign in the window. Their stomachs rumbled. What they wouldn't give for those prunes and toast!

For several days they wandered from one restaurant to another nearly begging for work. Occasionally a manager took pity on them and let them wait tables during the rush. But most days Norm and Margaret went to classes hungry. It was hard to concentrate and almost impossible to study when their stomachs felt so hollow.

Norm thought about going back to his family's farm. At least he'd have a full belly. There were eggs in the hen house, potatoes in cold storage, and canning jars filled with preserved summer vegetables. In the city, if he wanted to eat, he needed money.

Then a friend gave Norm a whole roll of coupons to the White Castle hamburger joint. That was where well-off college kids hung out. The coupons looked suspicious. Norm wondered if they were fake, but he was too hungry to worry about it.

Norm had never had a hamburger before, and certainly not one served seconds after it had been ordered. But for three coupons and ten cents Norm got three small hamburgers and a bottle of milk. He and Margaret lived off White Castle burgers for weeks. When the roll of coupons ran out, Norm again thought about quitting school and going home.

One night a friend from forestry class who served meals at a university sorority dining room told Norm the sorority was hiring. Norm raced over to the sorority house before anyone else could snag the job. Again, Norm would work for food, but this time it was ALL YOU CAN EAT!

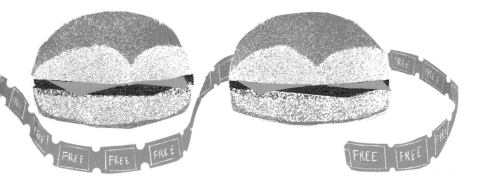

Wrestling with Hunger

In Norm's junior year, the wrestling coach quit. The team had been struggling, but being on a losing team was better than being on no team at all. Norm had an idea. Why not ask Coach Bartelma to come to Minnesota? As smooth as a diplomat, Norm helped bring his high school wrestling coach to the university. Soon enough, the team was on a winning streak.

Norm had never had trouble staying within his proper weight class, but for one match, Coach assigned Norm to a lower weight class. Norm put himself on a strict diet for a week. It was particularly hard with his all-he-could-eat waiter job. He stopped drinking water and spent hours at the gym sitting in the sweat box. Limiting his food made him cranky. He even snapped at Margaret.

The day of the big match, one extra pound stubbornly clung to his wiry body. As Norm sat in the sweat box, Coach joked about how lazy he was just sitting there.

Norm didn't laugh. He fumed inside.

Trying to keep his cool, Norm stepped out of the box.

A fellow wrestler tapped him on the shoulder. "Let's see how you've done, Norm."

Norm clenched his fists and swung around. "Take your hands off me," he snarled, "or I'll break your arm."[29]

Coach Bartelma jumped in to pull the two wrestlers apart.

Later, Norm made his weight class and won the match. But he could not celebrate. He'd let Hunger get the better of him. He thought

Marrying Margaret

After a summer job monitoring forest fires in Idaho, Norm proposed to Margaret. They married in 1937 in her brother's home near the university, and moved into Margaret's small apartment. Margaret quit school and took a job as a junior proofreader at a publisher's office, and Norm finished his forestry degree.

> **"A hungry man is worse than a hungry beast."**

about the men at the milk strike. "A hungry man is worse than a hungry beast." He just never thought it could happen to him.

Stakman Lights a Spark

An announcement posted on a campus bulletin board caught Norm's eye. "The Little Enemies that Destroy our Crops." The speaker, campus Professor Elvin C. Stakman, was the Dean of the university's Plant Pathology department. Stakman was renowned for his studies on grain crops. Norm had also heard Professor Stakman was a good speaker, so, on a whim, he attended the program.

Norm had studied tree diseases in forestry class, but he hadn't thought much about the diseases that attacked farmer's crops even though potato blight caused his great grandparents to leave their homeland. That was the point of Stakman's lecture. Crop diseases were "voracious destroyers of man's food," he said. "Biological science, crop disease, soil infertility, human population, and world hunger are all interwoven." That night in the Northrop Auditorium, "Stakman lit up the skies" for Norm. His mind reeled with the information he learned.

FOOD FOR THOUGHT

PLANT PATHOLOGY

The study of plant diseases: their causes, effects, spread, and treatments.

Stakman focused on one type of fungus called rust, which he warned "is a shifty, changing, constantly evolving enemy. We can never lower our guard. And we must fight them by all means open to science."[33]

Over dinner, Norm repeated snippets of Stakman's lecture to Margaret. Something about the topic really hit home for Norm. A light deep inside him clicked on and burned bright. Farming, food, helping people—the very things he'd been brought up to value combined with science. Ideas circled in his head like puzzle pieces. He didn't know yet how to put the pieces together, but he was determined to figure it out.

A New Path

Norm was almost finished with his forestry degree when he decided to stay at the university and get a graduate degree. This time, Norm chose to learn plant pathology with Professor Stakman.

Stakman's teaching style involved hands-on science. He took his students out into the university's fields where forty acres of diseased plants wilted and wheezed with all sorts of diseases: rust, mildew, blight, smut, scab, and blast. Like a medical student visiting patients in a hospital, Norm answered Stakman's questions, diagnosed plants, and offered treatments. Stakman routinely challenged what Norm thought and why he thought it.

Norm learned how to spot early signs of disease and how to identify them under a microscope. He learned how to breed healthier plants too, following the textbook tradition of growing plants in their specific locations according to the proper length of day and appropriate length of season.

Professor Stakman impressed upon Norm that when dealing with farm crops, the stakes were extremely high. A misdiagnosis could allow a bacteria or fungus to explode into an epidemic and wipe out crops from one state to the next in a festering tidal wave. Once disease drowned grain supplies, Hunger snuck in. Plant disease and Hunger worked a double punch:

BAM! Disease hit the plants.

BAM! Hunger hit the people.

In the fall of 1941, The DuPont Corporation offered Norm a job in their offices in Delaware. Norm couldn't believe it. He hadn't even finished his degree. But Stakman had written him a glowing recommendation.

Norm would work in the agricultural division as head of a

Norma Jean

N orm and Margaret had a lovely apartment in Wilmington, Delaware. On September 27, 1943, Margaret and Norm welcomed their first child, a girl named Norma Jean, Jeanie for short.

biochemical laboratory and earn $2,800 a year. That was more money than he'd ever dreamed of making!

What an opportunity! On December 1, 1941, the young couple packed their Pontiac with what few belongings they had and left Minneapolis. Before major highways existed, it took an entire week to drive across half of the country.

On December 7, Norm and Margaret passed through Philadelphia where, strangely, dozens of people were huddled in doorways. Folks were leaning out of windows as if waiting to hear news. What news? From the somber expressions on people's faces, Norm guessed it was not good. At a street corner, a newspaper boy waved a special edition. Norm rolled down his window. "Pearl Harbor bombed!" the boy bellowed. Japan had attacked Hawaii. The United States was now at war.

War Work

Norm's agricultural job at DuPont quickly turned into military assistance. The government classified him "essential to the war effort," which meant he was more useful doing research at DuPont than being drafted as a soldier.

Nearly every day, a military officer brought Norm a problem to solve. The Marines needed a waterproof adhesive to keep cartons of food secure; another officer asked him to find a way to prevent all of their equipment from getting moldy. In the tropics, fuzz was growing over binoculars, eating holes in tents, and ruining medical supplies. Norm developed cellulose acetate, a thin clear film that, if made into a sack, kept things dry. Norm learned to work fast. He started with what he knew, then used his imagination and improvised. Norm called his process "speed science."

Lasting Ideas

Many of the innovations Norm worked on at DuPont are still in use today. Candy wrappers, rain coats, umbrellas, and wrinkle-free shirts all contain some form of Norm's cellulose acetate. And most packaging is glued with Norm's waterproof adhesive.

In 1944, the federal government released Norm from special duty. He was free to stay at DuPont and earn a lot of money, or he could accept another job offer, one that would take him to the middle of nowhere where he'd make little money working extremely hard to solve an impossible problem.

How could Norm resist?

PLANTING HOPE

"We will have to do the best we can with what we have."[34]

The surprising job offer came from George Harrar who worked for the Rockefeller Foundation, one of the largest humanitarian organizations in the world. Harrar asked Norm to join a partnership that had formed between the Rockefeller Foundation and the Mexican government. Mexico's population was rapidly growing, but their food production was not. This new partnership pledged to help farmers grow more food.

The light inside Norm flashed brighter. Helping farmers, growing food, feeding people? That was exactly what Norm wanted to do. Although Margaret would miss Norm mightily, she knew this was the opportunity he needed. This was a chance for Norm to make a difference in the world.

Road Trip

On September 11, 1944, Norm packed up the old Pontiac and set out across the country once more, this time taking the southern route to Mexico. At almost every intersection the desire to turn back was great—Jeanie was only a year old. But he kept going. Keeping to the forty-mph speed limit, Norm figured it would take at least six days to reach his destination.

Nearing Mexico City, he pulled out his directions and found the office of the Rockefeller Foundation housed in a whitewashed building in San Jacinto. Norm climbed three flights to the small cluster of rooms where Harrar worked. The American crew of the Mexican Agricultural Program (MAP) included Ed Wellhousen, a corn and bean specialist, and William Colwell, who studied soil. Norm would work with wheat, or *trigo* in Spanish.

Harrar explained that Norm would be working at a research facility in nearby Chapingo to improve Mexican crops, train Mexican scientists, and teach local farmers in the Bajio about new technology, wheat-planting techniques, and fertilizers. The Bajio region, northwest of Mexico City, was one of the nation's wheat-growing districts. It was also one of the poorest regions in the country. Harrar challenged the three scientists: "Make Mexico capable of feeding itself."

That was a tall order. Norm wondered if he'd made a huge mistake. How could he train Mexicans? He didn't even speak Spanish!

Good Deeds

Businessman John D. Rockefeller established The Rockefeller Foundation in 1913 "to promote the well-being of mankind throughout the world." The Mexican Agricultural Program (MAP) was its first international venture.

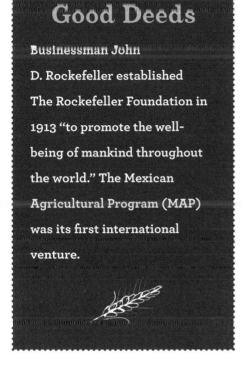

Chapingo

The next day, Norm and his colleagues drove twenty-five miles east to the research facility. The Mexican government had granted the Rockefeller team 150 acres of Chapingo farmland owned by the National Agricultural School. The only building was a small storage shed Ed Wellhousen had built the year before. Its black tar paper roof sheltered the dirt floor, and all around the shed were plots of rusty wheat, wilted corn, and bean plants so riddled with insects the leaves looked like lace. Flat and desolate, even weeds struggled to survive.

Norm didn't see a laboratory or a greenhouse or any equipment. "This was the first inkling that raising crops in Mexico might differ from anything we'd expected," Norm said. "Suddenly it seemed we shouldn't be so sure of ourselves."[36]

Their first task was preparing the site for planting. How would they orient the rows? Where would waterlines or drainage ditches lie? Norm had learned surveying in forestry school, so he was the one to lay lines for fences, roads, and drainage. Soon they had an orderly plan mapped out. The men dug ditches, set posts for fences, and began clearing the land of weeds. With no equipment other than shovels and rakes, it was backbreaking work. What they needed was a tractor. Because this was still wartime, all U.S. tractors were reserved for the military, but someone mentioned seeing a tractor graveyard behind the bank in a nearby town.

Norm and Wellhousen raced over to pick through the rusty carcasses. Chassis, exhaust pipe, worn tires—most of the equipment was beyond repair, but they struck gold when they hauled out two TD9 International bulldozers. They weren't tractors, but they were heavy and powerful machines they could use. They were also broken. Nobody on the team knew how to fix the engines, so they hired a mechanic who worked on tanks for the Mexican Army. For days Norm dug, raked, and hoed by hand while the mechanic dismantled the engines. He laid every part out on the grass.

Soon there were fewer parts on the grass and more in the dozers. Then one day the mechanic hoisted himself into the driver's seat of one of the dozers, opened the choke, and pulled the throttle. The engine roared to life, belching years of rust and neglect. Norm and the others whooped and hollered. Now they could get some *real* work done and make Chapingo look like a real experiment station.

Struggling to Survive

To learn more about Mexico's farming problems, Norm toured the Bajio. All the farms looked similar: squat thatch-roofed shacks, scrawny chickens, and even scrawnier children skittering through

yards of hardpacked dirt. Homes lacked electricity and running water.
Women walked for miles to pump dirty water out of the nearest well,
and children were dying from diseases that were treatable in
other countries.

With the help of an interpreter, Norm spoke with lots of farmers
who planted wheat by first poking holes in the ground with sharp
sticks. A son or daughter walked behind, dropping a seed into
each hole. If the farmer was lucky, there was an ox to pull a rickety
cultivator. It could have been a reenactment from medieval times.
When Norm looked at these men, however, he saw his father and
grandfather. These men were just family farmers too, working day by
day to feed their children.

As he traveled through the Bajio, Norm recorded his
observations in a small notebook. He noted the makeup of the soil,

which was as poor as the people. He saw that growing the same crop year after year had drained nutrients from the soil. Most farmers knew nothing about fertilizer, nor could they afford it. They also didn't trust fertilizer because their government promoted it. Norm jotted down the average rainfall, whether a farmer irrigated or not, and how they planted their fields. Farmers in the Bajio planted several kinds of wheat all mixed together like wildflowers on a hill. One *campesino* explained that planting the seeds far apart slowed the spread of stem rust, but still Norm saw the telltale red spots of rust everywhere he went.

The Bajio farmers also planted winter wheat even though the climate was more suited to growing wheat in the summer. Stem rust was more active in the summer months, explained a farmer. Norm noticed that it didn't really seem to matter what time of year the farmers planted; all too often the rust snuck in

Campesinos

When Mexico's lengthy civil war ended in 1920, the new government redistributed land so large tracts once held by the wealthy were divided into smaller units and given to farmers or campesinos. Unfortunately, the lots were often too small to sustain a family, and the soil lacked nutrients. The poor uneducated farmers often didn't have the skills to make their barren plots profitable. By 1943, the Mexican population had grown, but the country couldn't grow enough food to sustain its people.

anyway just before spring harvest. Stem rust was such a concern some campesinos refused to water their crops for fear of encouraging the fungus, which preferred warm, wet conditions. Norm thought this approach was like trying to prevent a heart attack by starving yourself.

During his travels, Norm's stomach seized up. Maybe he was feeling sympathy pains with the poor people of the Bajío, or maybe it was the dirty water and bad food that left him nauseated and sweating in his sleeping bag. For weeks he gritted his teeth as he rattled down rutted roads and up into the mountains.

In a letter to Margaret, Norm wrote, "These places I've seen … are so poor and depressing. The earth is so lacking in life force; the plants just cling to existence. They don't really grow; they just fight to stay alive…. Can you imagine a poor Mexican guy struggling to feed his family? I don't know what we can do to help these people, but we've got to do something."[37]

The Enemy

From all he'd seen, Norm knew that the biggest problem wheat farmers faced was the stem rust fungus. The "shifty, changing, constantly evolving enemy," Professor Stakman had spoken about in his lecture was now Norm's number one enemy in Mexico.

Rust fungus had been destroying wheat crops for more than 8,000 years when people first started to farm, and wheat farmers have wrestled with rust ever since. They have altered planting times, ripped out rust-riddled host plants called barberry bushes, and even prayed to rust gods. Now it was Norm's turn on the mat.

Professor Stakman's words echoed in Norm's head: "We can never lower our guard. We must fight rust by all means open to science." Norm was ready. But he couldn't do it alone. His first move was to assemble a team.

Summer and Winter Wheat

In many places around the world, farmers grow wheat in the summer. This summer wheat, or *trigo de verano,* grows quickly and is harvested in the fall. Winter wheat, *trigo de invierno,* is planted in October or November before a heavy frost. The seeds sprout, then remain dormant throughout the cold months. When the weather warms, the plants begin to grow again and can be harvested in the spring. Winter wheat can't flower unless it experiences a period of cold. This process is called vernalization (*vernal* meaning *spring*).

STEM RUST

Stem rust is a parasitic fungus that feeds off of wheat to survive. But that is only one part of its life cycle. It also harbors in barberry bushes, and during the winter months it lays dormant in Southern states and Central America. When conditions are wet and warm, the fungus releases thousands of microscopic spores that hitch a ride on the wind. Spores land on healthy wheat stalks and carve out blood-red pustules that weaken the stems and kill the wheat. Each pustule also contains thousands of spores which then spread from plant to plant, field to field, farm to farm.

Borlaug's Boot Camp

Part of MAP included training Mexican agronomy students, or *agronomos*. When the first two students, Pepe and José, arrived from the local National Agricultural School, Norm instantly saw a problem. Their suits and ties made them look more like government pencil pushers than agronomy students. Clearly, they were not dressed for the kind of training Norm had in mind. He planned to teach like professor Stakman, and take his students out to the field to let them see, feel, and smell the crops. "Being an agricultural scientist is being a worker who is not afraid to get his hands in the dirt," he said.[39]

Norm gestured to his own dirty work shirt, khaki pants, and well-worn work boots, and then questioned their Sunday best.

Pepe, who spoke English, explained that scientists in Mexico were highly regarded and it would be inappropriate to be seen wearing the common clothes of a laborer.

How could a scientist help farmers, Norm asked, if he did not understand the job of the farmer? "The only way you can teach them to do this is to do it yourself. You've got to work harder, sweat more, get dirtier, right beside them in the field."[40] And no one worked harder than Norm. He was always first in the field at dawn, and the last one to leave at night. He'd even work by the light of the moon as long as he could see his wheat stalks.

After an uncomfortable day sweating in suits and ties, Pepe and Jose arrived the next day in work shirts, khaki pants, and work boots.

Every time new recruits arrived, Norm gave the same lecture, and soon everyone came prepared, although some hid their work clothes in sacks so people on the bus wouldn't mistake them for field hands. Over the years, many of Norm's students said that his training was like being in the Peace Corps and Marine boot camp at the same time.

> ❝
> **"The only way you can teach them to do this is to do it yourself. You've got to work harder, sweat more, get dirtier, right beside them in the field."**[40]

Survival of the Fittest

In the spring of 1945, Norm shocked the local farmers by planting summer wheat. His trainees tried to explain to *el profesor* that this was a bad idea. The foreman at Chapingo said, "But Borlaug, señor, no wheat is planted here in the summer. The rain and heat and the rust will kill it. You will waste time and work, *patrón.*"[41]

That was the point. Norm welcomed the rust. He and his students planted 8,000 different varieties of Mexican wheat and almost 600 varieties from the United States to see what effect rust had on them, more than 100,000 seeds in all. Norm knew most of the plants would die in this kind of survival-of-the-fittest type of mass planting, but he also hoped his efforts would reveal one or two wheats that had a built-in resistance to the fungus. Those wheats would be the foundation for his breed-a-better-wheat project.

They planted ten to fifteen seeds in hundreds of short rows. Each type of wheat had a code number Norm kept track of in a loose-leaf binder. By the time they were finished, they had five miles of rows.

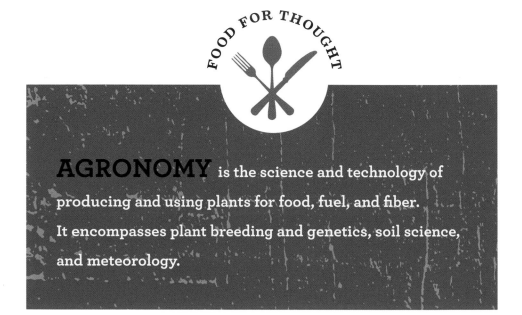

FOOD FOR THOUGHT

AGRONOMY is the science and technology of producing and using plants for food, fuel, and fiber. It encompasses plant breeding and genetics, soil science, and meteorology.

Within two weeks the first seedlings poked their heads through the soil. All 100,000 plants needed to be inspected for signs of rust. Norm and his men looked for black blotches, and oval orange spots called pustules. They felt for rough patches where a pustule was forming, and sniffed for the rancid odor of rot.

Leaf by leaf.

Plant by plant.

Row by row.

Norm recorded everything in his loose-leaf binder.

At noon one day, Norm took a break. He placed his notebook on a stool at the end of a row, then flipped a second stool and placed it on top to keep the notebook in place. He pulled off his ball cap, pushed back his sweat-slicked hair, and trudged to the cool of a shade tree. There he offered up sandwiches to his team. He always brought more than he could eat just so he could share. Beyond the tree's circle of shade, the sun's heat stirred up a column of hot air. It started to spin. The dust devil whirled and swirled across the field kicking up dirt and leaves. It was headed straight for Norm's notebook.

Stiff and sore, Norm raced into the field. Could he get there before the dust devil?

WHEAT WHISPERER

"When wheat is ripening properly, when the wind is blowing across the field, you can hear the beards of the wheat rubbing together.... It is a sweet whispering music that once you hear, you never forget."[42]

The mini tornado spun faster. Before Norm could rescue his precious notes, the dust devil swept up the top stool. "I stared in horror as the notebook came free and lifted into the air. It went up and up and was high above us when the binding opened and pages blasted out like confetti from a circus cannon."[43]

All that work.

All that data.

Gone.

Norm posted a reward for returned pages, but few were found. It was like he was six years old again, battling that blizzard. Only this time, instead of jeopardizing his schoolmates' feet with frostbite, he jeopardized Mexico's wheat research. Norm always used bound notebooks after that.

Casa de Borlaug

While alone in Mexico, Norm's home base was in the dingy Hotel Geneva in Mexico City. But Margaret and Jeanie were making plans to join him, so Norm found a large two-bedroom apartment a few blocks from the other Rockefeller Foundation families.

Almost immediately Margaret set to work cleaning and furnishing the apartment. She learned to navigate the colorful outdoor market, choose the right chilies, and prepare new foods. Jeanie thrived in the sunshine, picking up Spanish from the kids in the neighborhood. Although Norm now had someone to come home to, his work at Chapingo still took him away from dawn to dusk. Occasionally on a Saturday, Margaret packed a picnic lunch and she and Jeanie joined Norm at Chapingo. Jeanie raced up and down rows of wheat, never knowing just how important her father's work would become.

Five Miles a Day

The tedious plant inspection focused Norm's mind on nothing but rust. He and his team got used to flies buzzing around their heads and became numb to mosquitoes biting their necks. They ignored the no-see-ums, gnats, and tiny flies that drank so much blood they rolled off the men's arms, too fat to fly. Dust driven by the wind stuck to their sweaty skin giving them a sickly pale cast.

When Norm felt they weren't making enough headway, he dragged a sleeping bag out to the research facility and slept in the tar-paper shack. This way he could be in the fields at daybreak when it was cool and before the insects attacked. Although he missed Margaret and Jeanie, he was too exhausted in the evenings to drive home. He barely had enough energy to heat up a can of stew or beans before crawling into bed.

From sunrise to sunset, Norm lived with wheat. The more he worked with it, the more he learned. Each wheat stalk spoke to him. Each had a unique personality. Some were weak and wimpy, others were bold. "In a strange way the plants explained themselves … not by sound but by look, color, feel; the height and angle of their leaves; the size and hue of the surface; the size, appearance, and weight of the seeds; the spread and depth of their roots."[44] He could tell at a glance which variety he held. Even the sound of the wind through ripening stalks revealed vital information. Norm was becoming a true expert, and years later, newspaper reporters would call him "the wheat whisperer."

> **"Wheat itself was becoming a person."**[45]

If a damaged plant was found, it was ripped out by the roots. Soon, the field looked like the toothless smile of an old man. Norm was looking for the healthiest wheat possible. A sign of disease meant that a particular plant didn't have built-in resistance to rust. Only the healthiest plants survived until the next inspection. By the end of the first year, almost every single wheat plant had been yanked from the ground. Only four remained: Frontero, Supremo, Red Kenyan, and White Kenyan. These wheats would be multiplied to provide seed for farmers.

Match Making

In 1945, when Norm started his wheat breeding program, the science of genetics was just getting started. Nobody knew what DNA (deoxyribonucleic acid) was, or that genes controlled the physical characteristics of all living things. All Norm knew was that by carefully selecting one parent plant that had disease resistance and another parent that produced a lot of grain, he could potentially produce an offspring both disease-resistant *and* high-yielding.

Wheat is self-pollinating, which means wheat plants have both male and female parts. To breed the wheat, Norm had to wait until

July when male flowers formed on the wheat plants. Like a father who pre-arranges his child's marriage, he'd already figured out which plants to pair up. The four rust-resistant varieties would be combined with other wheats that would hopefully provide equally beneficial characteristics like larger grains or more seed heads.

The next step was the wedding. Norm stuffed his pockets with all the tools he'd need for the "mind-warpingly tedious" breeding process: scissors, pen, small envelopes, and paperclips. He hung a string around his neck from which dangled a fine-tipped tweezer. Then he headed out to the fields, followed by his students.

Norm first showed the men how to make one plant solely female. Gently holding the head of a wheat plant, he painstakingly tweezed apart each floret to reveal the male part of the plant called the *anthers* With the precision of a surgeon, Norm pulled out the three anthers which were as small as grains of sand on a hair-thin stalk.

To prevent any stray pollen from contaminating the plant, he placed a slim envelope over the stalk and secured it with a paperclip. In a few days, the female part of the plant called the *pistil* would be ready for pollination.

Norm then tweezed open the chosen "male" parent plant to expose its yellow anthers. Exposed to the heat of the sun, the anthers puff and push up. Once open, the plant must be crossed quickly before the heat damages the pollen. Like handling a bomb, Norm removed an anther, took it over to the "female" plant, opened the envelope, and twirled the anther inside the envelope to release the pollen. He replaced the paperclip, noted the crossbreeding, or cross, on the tag, and moved on to the next pair. Norm and his small crew worked quickly. There were hundreds of crosses to make in a short amount of time before the wheat matured and released its own pollen.

Most breeders crossed only ten or twenty plants, as if hoping to hit a bullseye with one throw of a dart. Norm knew the rules of plant breeding, he just didn't believe they were correct. He preferred to follow his own instincts and let wheat lead the way. Norm would throw a barrelful of darts at his target. The more crosses he and his students created, the greater their chances of finding a rust-resistant, high-yielding wheat. He would do this year after year, and by 1952, Norm would log in more than 6,000 crosses.

——————————— **66** ———————————

"Crossbreeding is a hit-or-miss process ... There is only one chance in thousands of ever finding what you want, and actually no guarantee of success at all."[47]

———————————————————————

WHEAT GENES

People first domesticated wheat about 9,000 years ago. Maybe its long history has something to do with its complex DNA. Wheat has five times more genetic material than humans have, and in 2018, for the very first time, wheat DNA was successfully mapped by an international team of 200 scientists. The map pinpoints where all of the 107,000 genes and more than four million genetic markers are located on the plant's twenty-one chromosomes.

Bird Boys

In the middle of the growing season, Norm noticed a few sparrow-sized birds snacking in the wheat field. He didn't think much of it. He liked birdsong, and often sang along with the *chanate* bird as he worked.

But soon an entire migrating flock descended on the wheat field. Norm and his team watched in horror as hundreds of hungry seed-eaters snipped off one grain after another. If they didn't do something quickly, they wouldn't have any seed left. All that back-breaking work would be flying north in the bellies of those birds!

Norm hired three young boys from a nearby village to act as boisterous scarecrows. At first the boys were quiet and shy around this strange English-speaking professor. Then the oldest introduced himself as Reyes Vega.

"Well, Reyes, you and your brothers do a good job. Come every morning," Norm said. "Okay?"[48]

"Okay, *Señor.*"

For three pesos a week, Reyes and his brothers ran barefoot through wheat as tall as they were. To Norm it looked like three straw hats dancing atop the wheat stalks. To scare the birds away, the boys threw dirt, waved sticks, and shouted Spanish words Norm could only guess at.

Like the wheat, the boys grew under Norm's care. They seized every opportunity to improve themselves. They followed Norm, soaking up everything he said. While Norm was pulling the anthers from a floret, Reyes asked what he was doing. Norm explained how the plant had both male and female parts, and why he had to remove the male parts in order to breed it with another plant.

"Can I try?" Reyes asked.

SPEED SCIENCE

"To [heck] with the extra work and strain.
It's got to be done, and I believe I can do it."[49]

Norm had a busy schedule and a lot of plants to prepare, but he lifted the string from around his neck and placed the tweezers in Reyes's hand. There was always time for learning.

The boy's slim fingers worked quickly, and soon he was as adept as Norm. From then on, Reyes worked side by side with Norm and the university students.

One day Reyes surprised Norm by trying something new. Instead of tediously tweezing apart the floret to reveal the anthers, Reyes simply snipped the top of the floret just above the anthers. Now he could see the anthers clearly and pull all three out in one motion. Norm looked on in amazement. Why hadn't he ever thought of that? Reyes's shortcut saved the team hundreds of hours of work.

Another time while Norm and Reyes prepared the "male" parent plants, Reyes clipped the top of the floret, then stuck the stem in the ground. Under the heat of the direct sun, the anthers quickly puffed and turned bright yellow. Now when Reyes twirled it over the female, a thick layer of pollen covered the pistil. Reyes's improvements made Norm proud. They were more efficient, saved time, and increased their success rate.

Norm supported his "bird boys" just as fiercely as George Champlin had supported him. Norm and the other scientists set up a school fund for the boys, and insisted they receive the same pay as the university trainees who did the same work.

Several of the boys went on to college, and Norm eventually promoted Reyes to superintendent of the Chapingo research center. Reyes managed planting, weeding, and harvest, and maintained accurate records.

Years later Norm said, "That's one of the best things I was ever involved in. The boys were among our greatest successes … they had the makings of champions."[50]

Going Rogue

After cross-breeding thousands of plants, Norm and his team waited. It took an entire growing season to see the results of Norm's match-making. With a single growing season per year, it would typically take ten to fifteen years before a new useful variety appeared. All summer as Norm inspected the crops, he wondered, How can I speed this up? What if I grew two crops a year?

Mexico had three main wheat-growing areas: The Bajio, where Norm was working; a small area north of the Bajio called La Laguna;

and a large area much farther north called the Yaqui Valley in the Sonora region. The three areas had completely different climates. Norm wondered what might happen if he planted a summer crop in the Bajio, then transferred his best rust-resistant wheats to the Yaqui Valley to grow in the winter? Conceivably, that could cut the breeding time in half.

There was only one problem. The Mexican government gave the U.S. team permission to work only in the Bajio. Norm's boss, Harrar, refused to risk having the whole project shut down for Norm's crazy idea.

Norm knew he was going against everything he had been taught. Every plant breeding text book insisted that breeding research be conducted in the same environment in which the plants would be farmed. Plants couldn't be cultivated in a strange location, in a different climate, or at the wrong time of year.

But why not? If there was a chance to speed up the process, Norm owed it to the people of Mexico to try. Those who were starving didn't have ten to fifteen years to wait for a better wheat to come along. Every chance Norm got, he hammered Harrar for permission to take seeds north to the Yaqui Valley. I'll do all the work myself, he promised. It won't cost the foundation anything extra. Norm would not give up. Finally, Harrar caved in. Norm could go. But only for one season. And only if he kept it a secret from the main offices of the Rockefeller Foundation.

The Yaqui Valley

In November 1946, Norm flew north with a sack full of seed. The rickety six-seater plane bumped and clattered down a dirt runway outside of Cuidad Obregon, a desert town that reminded Norm of an old western movie set.

Norm hitched a ride twenty-five miles to the abandoned experiment station where he would work. The place hadn't been used for more than ten years. Wind and sun had beaten up the buildings. There was no electricity, no telephone, no running water. Roofs leaked and windows were broken. Wild grasses had reclaimed the surrounding fields, weeds clogged drainage ditches, and farm equipment lay abandoned. "I never saw a more dismal scientific facility."[51]

It was nearly sunset when Norm arrived, so he chose a scruffy-looking storage shed for his bedroom. He ate a can of beans he'd brought in his backpack, and as darkness closed around him, he climbed into his sleeping bag. "During the night live rats ran over the bedroll. I pulled a coat over my head but slept very fitfully."[52]

Gringo Greetings

The next morning, Norm walked to the nearest farm and asked if he could borrow a tractor. Although his Spanish was still pitiful, he managed *"El tractor por favor?"* The farmer refused. Undeterred, Norm kept walking. Every farmer said no. It seemed nobody wanted to lend their most important piece of equipment to a strange *gringo* (English-speaking foreigner).

Norm returned to the research station and rummaged through the storage shed. He found rusted rakes, shovels in need of sharpening, and an old cultivator similar to the one Grandad Nels once used. Too bad Norm didn't have a horse to pull it. He dragged it out to the field anyway. Then he waited.

Soon the elderly caretaker arrived to make his rounds of the abandoned experiment station. Norm introduced himself, then led the caretaker out to the cultivator.

Norm pulled the harness straps over his shoulders, fastened the buckle across his chest, and gestured for the man to grab the handles and keep it going straight. Norm leaned forward and pulled. Slowly, the blade of the cultivator cut a furrow into the soil.

Every time Norm turned at the end of a row, he noticed a man watching from the road. After a while the man approached. His name was Aureliano Campoy and he lived one farm over. Campoy asked Norm what he was doing.

Norm explained he was breeding a better wheat.

Campoy squinted in suspicion, then nodded with approval.

"Glory be!" Norm wrote to Margaret that night. "He will let me have his tractor and some implements next weekend."[53]

With the borrowed tractor, Norm cut straight rows in record time. News of the wheat-breeding *gringo* spread, and soon other farmers and neighbors were dropping by. Mrs. Jones offered to drive Norm to town once a week, cook him dinner, and teach him Spanish. "On week nights," Norm said, "she invited me over and forced me to brush up my grammar. Drilled me so relentlessly I at last learned to communicate."[54]

Game Changer

Norm's plan to shuttle wheat seed back and forth from north to south twice a year was primarily to speed up the breeding process. He was also shattering the long-held principle that plants were hard-wired to grow in specific conditions and could not adapt.

When Norm planted seeds in the south, they experienced dry, infertile soils, longer periods of daylight, and an altitude of 8,000 feet above sea level. When he took the next generation's seeds north, the plants became used to an entirely different environment. In the north the soil was irrigated and fertile. It sat at sea level, and had a much shorter period of daylight. Only the plants that survived in both locations generated seed for the next round of what became known as shuttle breeding. Norm's wheat was adaptable. It was no longer limited to just the Bajio or just the Yaqui Valley.

Plants Tell Time

Photoperiodism is the physical response that a plant has to the amount of light or darkness it receives within a twenty-four-hour period. Certain light conditions can trigger a plant to flower. There are plants that prefer long days with lots of light, and some prefer short days. The black-eyed Susan, for example, seems to know when the longest day of the year is approaching and this triggers it to flower. Chrysanthemums, on the other hand, won't bloom until the days begin to shorten in the fall.

Scientists discovered a light-sensitive protein pigment called **phytochrome** that allows a plant to keep track of time. During daylight hours the pigment is considered active, turning inactive in complete darkness. Somehow plants are able to compare the amount of time the pigment has been active versus inactive, and "count" the hours as they tick by.

By exposing the wheat plants to two different environments, Norm created a wheat that didn't know how to tell time.

"Through the use of this technique, we developed high-yielding, day-length-insensitive varieties with a wide range of ecologic adoption and a broad spectrum of disease resistance—a new combination of uniquely valuable characters in wheat varieties."[55]

It's A Boy

On March 29, 1947, Margaret gave birth to a son whom they named Bill. Now that Norm worked two to three months a year up in the Yaqui Valley, he was away from home more than ever. Although Norm felt guilty, Margaret assured Norm his growing family was fine. The Rockefeller Foundation families lived close by, and she understood the gravity of Norm's work. Margaret plunged into the role of mother of two. She also led Girl Scouts and taught English at a private school in Mexico City.

Take it to the Farmer

Despite Harrar's misgivings, Norm continued shuttle breeding. In 1948, Norm was ready to share four new wheat varieties with the Mexican farmers. He named them Yaqui 48, Nazas 48, Chapingo 48, and Kentana 48. These wheats were not perfect, but they were a vast improvement over what farmers were currently planting. The sooner farmers planted the rust-resistant wheat, the sooner they could have healthier crops, healthier families, more income, and better lives.

In order to spread the word about his rust resistant, higher-yielding wheat, Norm hosted his first Farmers Field Day in the Yaqui Valley. Norm wrote advertisements, visited government officials, and spoke on local radio shows to promote the event. Flyers announcing "Farmers Field Day—Free Beer and Barbeque" papered every flat surface in Obregón.

Norm practiced a speech in Spanish, printed information sheets, and filled small sample bags of seed to hand out to interested farmers. His friend Campoy brought over his flatbed truck to use as a platform where Norm could address the audience, and Mrs. Jones set up tables and supervised the barbeque.

The morning of the Field Day the wheat gleamed in the sunshine. Norm was convinced each plot would show farmers the importance of proper watering, weed control, and sowing seeds at the right time, at the right depth and distance apart. How could any farmer pass up the opportunity to plant seed that would yield twice as much grain as in the past?

By noon only five farmers had shown up. A few more straggled in, but they ignored Norm. They preferred sampling the free beer. Although he was disappointed at the low turnout, Norm considered it a successful day. He managed to convince one farmer, Roberto Maurer, to grow the new seed. Now, he thought, the word will spread.

Fertilize!

After another year of shuttle breeding, Norm hosted a second Farmers Field Day in 1949. Sure enough, this time two hundred farmers crowded in to meet Norm and see an even better variety of wheat. This year Norm's focus was on the use of fertilizer. Mexican soil was worn out from decades of farming, and the soil needed to be revived.

Norm led the spectators from one small square test plot to another, each with varying amounts of fertilizer. It looked just like Mr. Schroder's experiments back in high school. As he had done in high school, Norm believed that these farmers would appreciate the difference fertilizer made. At the end of Norm's presentation, the crowd just stared at him in silence.

What had he done? Had he mistakenly insulted them in Spanish?

Finally, Jorge Parada stepped up. This experiment might work on the research station, the man said, but it wouldn't work on their farms. They didn't have poor soil. They didn't need fertilizer.

Norm's mouth hung open. How could they believe that? Why wouldn't they want to improve their soil? I'll prove it to you, Norm said. I will plant experimental plots at someone else's farm. Parada quickly volunteered his place.

Seeds of Hope

Norm never expected to encounter such resistance from farmers. He clearly had to go around to farms and, like a traveling salesman, convince the locals one by one. Day after day Norm drove through the countryside looking for rust-infested fields. When he found one, he tried to explain to the farmer he'd like to plant a new kind of wheat on their property so they could see how well it grew.

Norm managed to convince one farmer, but as he hooked up a steel-bladed cultivator, the man yelled, *Alto!* Stop! The metal will pull the heat from my soil, the *campesino* said. My crops won't grow!

Norm promised nothing bad would happen. He plowed a small patch and planted his wheat seed.

A few days later, Norm called on the farmer again. His heart sank when he saw cows stomping over the newly planted field. The cows, the farmer said, put heat back into the land.

On another trip to the Bajio, Norm stopped by a particularly rust-infested crop. From across the field the farmer called out. "What are you doing?" Norm braced himself for a confrontation. He took a deep breath and launched into his pitch about the new seed.

The farmer hurried over and grabbed Norm's arm. "You have to give me some," he pleaded.[56] He'd always had bad luck with wheat and was desperate for a good harvest.

Norm opened the back of his pickup truck, grabbed a bag of seed, and handed it to the man. Norm explained the best way to plant it and gave him fertilizer too.

The farmer took Norm's hand and kissed it. *Gracias!*

Norm was thankful too. Finally, he was gaining the farmers' trust.

Growing Gratitude

In the summer months, Norm worked at the Chapingo research station and with farmers in the Bajio. Each winter he hauled larger and larger amounts of seeds north to the Yaqui Valley. Eventually, there was too much seed to drag on a plane, so Norm piled it in the back of a pickup truck and he and a couple of men drove the 1,200 miles (2000 km) over unmarked dirt roads, into the mountains and down into the valleys. Once, he tried to avoid the most dangerous

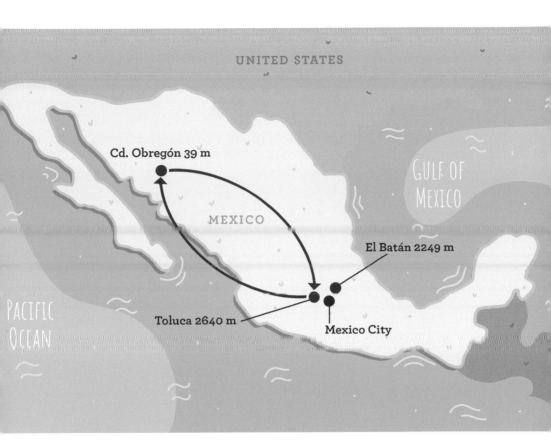

UNITED STATES

Cd. Obregón 39 m

GULF OF
MEXICO

MEXICO

El Batán 2249 m

PACIFIC
OCEAN

Toluca 2640 m

Mexico City

Shuttle breeding between Toluca and Obregon

river crossings by going through the United States. Authorities confiscated his equipment and made him late for planting season.

On another trip, a flood trapped Norm and three young *agronomos* in their station wagon. One of the *agronomos* was Ignacio Narvaez. His friends called him Nacho. This was Nacho's first trip with Norm. The men huddled in the station wagon while the water rose around them. "We were wet as sponges and had no way to dry off." The next day the four men managed to escape to a hotel. Nacho spied the piano in the lobby and sat down to play. "The tunes he coaxed from that battered old instrument were magical," Norm said.[57] Nacho had already impressed Norm with his hard work in the field, and, "Now he showed his talent to lift our spirits." Norm offered him a full-time job.

Norm continued to make these hazardous trips because they were worth it. Once, when traveling through the Bajio, a farmer stopped Norm's pickup. He hugged Norm. Then other farmers came out to shake the hand of the scientist who'd created a wheat that yielded three times more grain. Norm was delighted, but stunned at their show of gratitude. "It is a simple thing," a friend said. "They're saying thank you for having something to eat when the family would otherwise have been hungry!"[58]

Paper Pile-Up

Not everyone was pleased with Norm, however. Funding for the project was running low. Even though shuttle breeding was working, Rockefeller Foundation officials asked Norm to stop. Norm refused. He even threatened to quit. Reluctantly they let Norm continue, but insisted that he keep them informed of his work and results.

Norm's work ethic simply did not mesh with bureaucracy. He traveled thousands of miles several times a year, trained dozens of agronomy students, and monitored thousands of wheat plants. He didn't have time to write reports. Even so, administrators came close to firing Norm more than once over paperwork. When prodded he bellowed, "Do you want paper or bread?"

Too Much of a Good Thing

By 1950, Norm's best wheats were growing five to six feet tall. With added fertilizer to restore the soil the wheat heads swelled, yielding two to three times more grain. This was wonderful, but it also presented a new problem. A heavy wind could bend the towering stalks. Unable to hold the grain up, the stalks could crimp and the wheat heads jam or "lodge" in the soil. The farmer might be able to salvage some of the crop, but if the stalks broke, the grain withered away.

It had taken Norm years to create the high-yielding and rust-resistant wheat. It would take even more time to solve the problem of lodging. Where would he even begin?

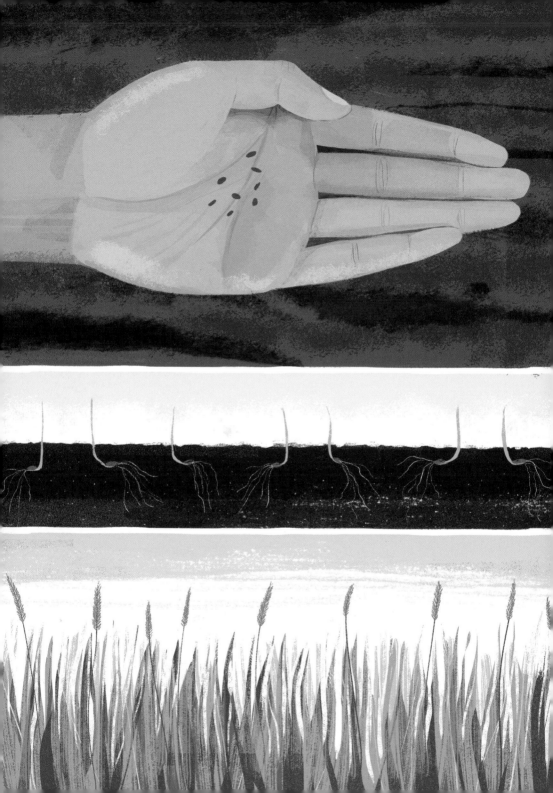

SEEDS OF THE FUTURE

> "There always seemed to be barriers beyond barriers.... But I could not give up trying to get past them because I could see the light shining under the door leading into that genetic storeroom."[59]

Norm knew he could create a smaller seed head that the long stalks could easily hold up, but that would mean less grain per plant. The farmers would revolt. Now that they'd experienced the joy of large successful harvests, they wouldn't want to give that up. Besides, Mexico was still not producing enough wheat to feed itself. Norm's only option was to create a shorter, stronger stalk that could hold up the heavy heads.

Norm had been wrestling with Mexico's wheat for six years and had developed several rust-resistant, high-yielding varieties, but now he had to add another characteristic into the mix. It was like starting over. No one knew how each characteristic would affect the other. Some plant breeders discouraged him. It was a waste of time, they said. Impossible. Crazy!

But Norm wouldn't give up. His new goal was to create a wheat that matured quickly, was rust resistant, and had short stiff stalks that could hold several grains per spikelet.

Mail-Order Mates

Norm wrote to universities, plant breeders, and even contacted the U.S. Department of Agriculture, which housed 30,000 types of wheat in the World Wheat Collection. He asked for samples of wheat that might have the potential for shorter stalks.

Envelopes arrived daily from around the world. All together, Norm and his team planted more than 20,000 kinds of wheat. Like an explorer feeling his way in the dark, he knew where he wanted to go, but the plants would not let him pass. None developed the kind of stalk he needed. Still, he would not quit. Even his crew had never seen him so focused.

Among the many envelopes was one sent by Orville Vogel of the U.S. Department of Agriculture. Inside, Norm found seeds of a dwarf wheat from Japan. Vogel said this breed, called Norin 10, grew only two feet tall. In 1953, Norm planted the dwarf wheat in the Yaqui Valley. That winter a new strain of rust attacked the field and killed every Norin 10 plant.

For the next two years, Norm and his team doggedly planted, inspected, discarded, and bred thousands of plants, but were no closer to their goal. It looked like maybe the other breeders were right.

SAVING SEEDS

Today, the largest wheat seed collection is housed in Mexico City at the *Centro Internacional de Mejoramiento de Maiz y Trigo* (CIMMYT) Germplasm Bank. More than 150,000 varieties collected from around the world are kept in vaults that could hold twice that amount. One vault is kept at zero degrees Fahrenheit, while long-term storage underground is a chilly -18°F. Preserved for the future of our food supply, the seeds are also studied and made available free for research and breeding programs.

Maybe a short, rust-resistant, high-yielding wheat was impossible. If only he had more of the Norin 10.

Maybe, just maybe, he did have more....

On a hunch, Norm searched around the old storage shed at Chapingo. There thumbtacked to the wall, along with dozens of other random dirty envelopes, was one labeled Norin 10. The same envelope Vogel had sent him two years earlier. Norm tipped the envelope, and eight seeds tumbled into his palm. Why he'd left eight seeds behind out of the dozens Vogel had sent him, Norm had no idea. Maybe he knew he would need them one day. Norm took the seeds back to the Yaqui Valley. "We'll take good care of these," he said. "In the final analysis we need only one seed—if it's the right seed."[60]

CIANO

In 1955, the Yaqui experimental station had undergone a change. Farmers and other members of the community who had prospered from Norm's work had raised money to upgrade the facility. It was now called the *Centro de Investigaciones Agricolas del Noroeste* (The Northeast Center for Agricultural Investigations)—CIANO for short. The center featured a laboratory, greenhouse, proper storage facilities, and a special plant protection room.

Norm took no chances with those eight Norin 10 seeds. He decided to vernalize them to make them *think* they'd gone through the winter. He moistened the seeds on a cotton cloth and put them in a cooler for six weeks. Then he planted each chilly seed in a separate pot. He placed them in the protected area so no rust spores could find them. Just to be sure, Norm wrapped them loosely in cotton cloth, and warmed them under grow lamps.

Throughout the winter he watched as the eight seeds sprouted and leaves emerged. They grew to be half as tall as regular wheat but developed more stalks per plant. Each stalk also held heads with more grain.

Let's Play Ball

Having a son brought out the kid in Norm. When Bill was about seven years old, Norm and another dad, John Niederhauser, a fellow researcher at Chapingo, formed the first Little League baseball in Mexico City. On Friday evenings, Norm left the wheat fields and drove home, sometimes up to six hours, depending on where he'd been working. Saturday mornings he'd gear up, put on his Aztec coaching cap, and he and Bill played ball.

The first year, only two teams of American boys played. The second year, the little league attracted dozens of local boys to form four teams—the Aztec, Maya, Toltec, and Metropolitan. Norm welcomed everyone. If a boy didn't have a glove, Norm always had extras to give away. If a boy couldn't get to the ball field, Norm made the rounds picking up and dropping off. Norm left no one out.

By 1956, there were three leagues in Mexico City, and other Mexican towns had started their own. In 1957, the Monterrey team from northern Mexico won the Little League World Series in Williamsport, Pennsylvania!

OUTBREAK

In 1954, a new kind of stem rust called 15B infected the United States and destroyed more than 300 million bushels of wheat. It moved north and killed 120 million bushels in Canada. Norm and his team recognized the urgency of finding a 15B-resistant wheat. The Rust Prevention Association was established, and Norm launched the International Spring Wheat Yield Nursery in Mexico. Thousands of varieties of wheat poured into the experimental station where it was planted and studied. Although many plant breeders kept their varieties private, Norm believed the only way to maintain a healthy food supply was to share the knowledge and the seed. Over the years more countries joined the effort. "This nursery was the vehicle through which the broadly adapted, high-yield, stem-rust-resistant dwarf wheat varieties spread around the world from Mexico."[61]

Just before the plants were fully mature, Norm chose eight rust-resistant wheats from his fields, and using Reyes's method removed the male anthers to prepare them for breeding. A few days later, the Norin 10 plants were ready. Norm clipped the spikelets and carried the plants outside. As soon as the pollen bloomed in the sun, Norm shook the Norin 10 pollen onto the waiting pistils, and hoped for the best.

Success!

In the fall of 1955, Norm harvested the wheat made from crossing Norin 10 with several Mexican wheat varieties. He collected 1,500 seeds and shuttled them to Chapingo to be planted and crossed again.

Ruthlessly inspecting the fields and ripping out the unacceptable plants, Norm grew closer to his ideal. Mixing the Norin 10 and Central American wheats were creating some startling results. Some of the varieties had six grains per spikelet rather than two. Others sprouted six or more stalks rather than two or three. Some wheats resisted the newest rust, and some had a reddish tint to the bran (the hard husk covering the kernel). Two plants in particular looked promising, Lerma Rojo and Sonora. Their stalks grew knee high and carried more grain than any previous variety. Norm was confident Mexican farmers would be delighted with the results.

He had always believed farmers should use the best seed available at any given time. In the late 1940s, Mexican farmers planted the seeds from Norm's early crosses. As the wheat improved, the amount of wheat Mexico produced grew. Despite the problems with lodging, growing Norm's taller rust-resistant, high-yielding wheat meant the country no longer had to import grain.

In 1956, Mexico announced for the first time in history it was producing enough wheat to feed its citizens. The seemingly impossible challenge Norm took on twelve years before—make Mexico feed itself—had been met. By breeding a better wheat, Norm had worked himself out of a job.

MAP was replaced by an international organization called the *Centro Internacional de Mejoramiento de Maiz y Trigo* (The International Corn and Wheat Improvement Center), or CIMMYT for short. The *agronomos* Norm had trained from the agricultural college, as well as Reyes Vega and the two other boys whose first job had been chasing away birds, would now take over Norm's wheat research. In January of 1960, Norm named Dr. Ignacio (Nacho) Narvaez the new director of CIANO. There was no one Norm trusted more with his pint-sized plants.

The thought of moving on was bittersweet. Norm was extremely proud of his students, and grateful to have been able to stave off Hunger and fill millions of Mexican bellies. However, Mexico had been the Borlaugs' home for nearly twenty years. Wheat had been Norm's life. Now what would he do?

YUCK OR YUM!

One critical characteristic of any wheat is good bake-ability. No matter how rust-resistant or high-yielding a variety was, no one would want it if it made awful bread. To test his wheats, Norm hired Eva Villegas. Working in a glorified garden shed, Eva milled a pound or two of grain and baked loaf after loaf of bread. She measured each loaf by height, texture, color, and taste.

Each year Eva tested thousands of wheat varieties. Only the best-tasting wheats went on to the next breeding round. Unfortunately, Norm and Eva discovered that short wheat made poor bread. Somehow the two characteristics were linked. They had to settle on a semi-dwarf wheat of medium height to get a loaf of bread as delicious as Norm's grandmother's.

HUNGER BOOM

"**Never think for a minute that we are going to build permanent peace in this world on empty stomachs and human misery. It won't happen, and the sooner our leaders at all levels of society reflect on that, the better.**"[62]

While Norm was improving Mexico's wheat supply, scientists in the United States and around the world were sounding an alarm.

"Ten persons are added each minute to the population of India, where fifteen percent of the earth's population is crowded into two point three percent of the world's area.... Officials estimate India's population will double in thirty years or less."
—*San Bernardino Sun*, March 6, 1958.[63]

"Sir Charles Darwin, physicist and grandson of author Charles Darwin says, 'However much food is produced, there will always be too many mouths to feed.'"
—*The New York Times*, December 3, 1959.[64]

"The Population Reference Bureau said today that unless population growth was controlled in some underdeveloped countries, world chaos would be inevitable."
—*The New York Times*, December 27, 1959.[65]

"Reports from all over India tell of shortages, hunger and even starvation. Unrest is mounting.… Fears are that, if something concrete is not done quickly … India may face catastrophe."
—*The New York Times*, August 1, 1960.[66]

After World War II, the Earth experienced a population boom. In a short span of twenty years, the human species had added one billion people to the planet! Many researchers worried food production could not keep up with baby production.

The amount of land suitable for farming is rather small. Most of the world is covered in water, ice, mountains, deserts, or cities. In order to feed more people, agriculturalists would have to find a way to grow more food on the same amount of land. Many scientists thought that was impossible, even though Norm was quietly increasing wheat yield every year. Books like *Our Plundered Planet* by Fairfield Osborn (1948) and a 1954 pamphlet called *The Population Bomb* by Hugh Everett Moore were predicting widespread famine across the world.

Sadly, in many countries, famine was already commonplace. India experienced famine once or twice a decade, with one of the worst famines occurring in 1943. Nearly three million people died from starvation and disease. Those who survived remained stunted and disabled for life. The lack of protein dulled a person's hair and tinged it red. Hunger shriveled a child's legs down to bony sticks and swelled her belly with fluids her cells were too weak to hold. Hunger killed one child out of every ten before the age of one and took the lives of many more before the age of four.

Assessing the Situation

To address the growing concern over food scarcity, in October 1945, the United Nations had created the Food and Agricultural Organization (FAO). In 1960, just as Norm was wondering what his next job would be, the FAO invited him to represent the Rockefeller Foundation on a team traveling to Asia, Africa, and the Middle East to survey the health of wheat and barley crops.

For three months, he and the other delegates bounced along dusty dirt roads past farmers in rock-riddled fields. The scene in many rural areas looked the same no matter what country they were in. Occasionally, a bullock with its ribs showing pulled a rickety cultivator, a barefoot boy following behind shouting commands.

Most of the people Norm met lived in mud hut villages and earned less than ten cents a day. He spoke with families whose children as young as seven worked in the fields. At harvest time, women picked wheat by hand. "It gave me an undying admiration for the women in third-world countries who do such things every day," said Norm, "until they succumb at an early age to overwork."[67]

At each field, Norm inspected the sorry-looking wheat and jotted down the condition of the soil in a notebook. He also recorded the average rainfall and signs of disease. It was easy to see that weeds competed for what little nutrition the soil held, and that farmers let the monsoons decide how much or how little water fed their crops.

The most sophisticated farm tools he saw were hand-held sickles and the ox-drawn cultivator. It was if there had never been an industrial revolution. "They all stuck stubbornly to their ancient methods of agriculture," Norm said. "They seemed not to think about it. The way they took this enormous poverty clobbered my mind. It weighed down most of all on that poor, skinny farmer and his large family."[68]

In one of his notebooks he simply wrote: "humanity—frightening."[69]

The FAO team also visited each country's government offices. Almost immediately Norm understood that national and regional governments did not respect farmers. Officials were more interested in industry than in agriculture. Many of the agricultural scientists were even worse. They were more concerned about keeping their jobs than improving food production. Even in India, where the population was growing rapidly, mandates to increase food production came too slowly, if at all. It was as if politicians and academics didn't connect farming with food or with people.

Norm asked one agronomist why the agricultural agencies didn't give the farmers better crops. The scientist said they were afraid to, because then they would be blamed if their efforts failed. No one wanted to lose their jobs. India reminded Norm of his first encounters in Mexico—"impoverished soils, lack of science, a backward rural economy, a people wallowing in poverty of capital and ideas, and totally lacking in leadership—but it was on a much vaster scale." The Indian leaders "lacked courage, vision and ... had no sympathy or connection with the poor."[70]

The FAO trip ended in Rome. All the delegates were asked to write a report about what they saw. For several days, Norm sat sullenly in his hotel room staring at a blank page. It wasn't the paperwork he was upset about. He was angry and frustrated because, as he saw it, "Half of humanity was going to bed hungry. Their governments gave agriculture low priority.... How could all that be changed?"[71]

Norm's Plan

To clear his head, Norm walked through St. Peter's Square and sat on a bench to watch tourists posing for photos and children playing, their laughs echoing in the grand plaza. Norm thought about the children he had met on the trip. They seldom laughed. It was hard to laugh on an empty stomach.

Then Norm thought about Reyes, Nacho, and all his young *agronomos*. He could have never helped Mexico without them. Their training turned them into creative scientists willing to work with farmers and inspire politicians. Their energy transformed Mexican agriculture. That was it! With new purpose, Norm hurried back to his

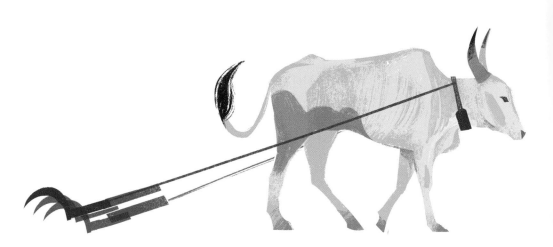

room, grabbed pen and paper, and dashed off his ideas.

"I propose the first order of priority should be the rapid, intensive, and practical training of a corps of dedicated young agronomists from each country willing to take part.... I further recommend that ... these young men be sent, for roughly a year, to the establishments in Mexico where so many young agronomists have already been trained in the new aggressive approach to modern agronomy."[72]

Norm offered to lead the training, and suggested that each country willing to take part receive seed to plant in experimental plots. Then the scientists could compare their traditional wheat to Norm's Mexican varieties. "On those hundreds of millions of rundown acres, scratched over by animal and human muscle power, in an industry dominated by the ox and the wooden plow, only new confidence and hope among the people can bring revival."[73]

Without bothering to type it out, Norm filed his report and headed home to his family in Mexico.

Stampede!

Norm returned to the Yaqui Valley just in time for the 13th Farmers Field Day. Nacho anticipated 3,000 visitors, and arranged for guests to tour the farm on trailers pulled by tractors. At each plot an *agronomo* was stationed to describe the wheat. The most important plot was the semi-dwarf wheat project. For several years, they had continued breeding the descendants of Norm's eight Norin 10 seeds, getting closer and closer to an ideal wheat that would solve the lodging problem. Nacho felt it was time to show them off.

Although the wheat carried twice as much grain as its taller cousins, Norm still wasn't sure if the wheat was ready to go public. He hoped to tweak it in the next round of cross breeding. He also worried that the semi-dwarf wheat might cause a ruckus among the farmers.

Nacho sent a few extra students to stand by the display of semi-dwarf wheat. Let no one off the trailers, he said. Farmers could look, but not touch.

The first tractor pulled up to the semi-dwarf wheat site. The *campesinos* craned their necks to look at the plot on display. At first the two rows of knee-high wheat looked like an immature crop. Then the farmers noticed the heavy seed heads bulging atop the compact stalks.

One by one farmers leaped off the trailer, swarming the field like

Reunion in Argentina

Knowing the semi-dwarf wheat was in good hands with Nacho, Norm accepted an invitation from the FAO to go to Argentina and help with their wheat. While there he read in the newspaper that fifteen United States governors were visiting nearby. Norm recognized a name. Before he left for work, he stopped by the governors' hotel and left his business card. When Norm returned to his motel later, a shiny black limousine was parked outside. For him! The driver waited while Norm changed out of his grimy clothes, then took him to the governor's ball.

Norm felt out of place standing in the receiving line with businessmen, politicians, and other dignitaries. He dutifully shook hands with each perplexed politician until he got to the governor of Idaho. Norm hadn't seen him since college. Robert E. Smylie. The boy who'd shared his cramped loft above his family's gas station.

Tears rolled down Smylie's cheeks as he gestured to the gold chandeliers and red velvet curtains. "Norm," Smylie said, "how on earth did we get to a point like this?"[74] Neither could have imagined that two scruffy kids from rural Iowa would grow up to make a real difference in the world.

locusts. The *agronomos* tried to push them away, but the farmers were seeing a miracle and they wanted a piece of it. Snapping off seed heads, they stuffed their pockets full.

Norm, watching from a distance, made no move to protect his plant-children. He did not say a word. He only smiled. He now knew that his vision for semi-dwarf wheat was the solution Mexican farmers had been waiting for.

Going Global

To Norm's great satisfaction the FAO liked his report and followed up on his suggestions. They invited impoverished countries to participate and within weeks the first trainees arrived from Pakistan, Egypt, Libya, Iraq, Iran, Syria, and Turkey. As they stepped off the bus, Norm welcomed them. "We're going to teach you how to be rebels. Not with guns and daggers, but with science and technology."[75] He also delivered his lecture about the importance of getting dirty, insisting the trainees work beside him in the field. "I deliberately make it tough on them…. We have to. They have got to learn to be tough and to rely on themselves when they get back to their own countries and start working on their crops."[76]

Over the heads of wheat, Spanish mingled with Arabic, Hindi, Urdu, and other languages as the trainees fingered wheat stems and examined leaves. Regardless of what language they spoke, they all listened for the whisper of one voice—wheat!

After several months, the trainees returned to their home

115

> **"Plants will talk to you if you listen. But they won't shout. You'll never hear them if you stay in an air-conditioned office."** [77]

countries with samples of wheat seed, including one that had not been named yet. It only had a number, 8156. In the semi-dwarf breeding program, it was the result of the 8156th cross. In the coming weeks they would plant and grow this wheat in their own test plots following Norm's strict instructions. Hopefully, at least one variety would perform well and spark a resurgence in that nation's wheat supplies.

India Calling

Though India needed Norm's help, its government did not send a single trainee. Instead, India decided to continue their reliance on humanitarian aid from the United States and other nations. But after ten years of relief, world leaders were putting pressure on India to increase their agriculture.

Through CIMMYT's International Rust Prevention Initiative, India had received samples of Norm's semi-dwarf seeds in 1961. The agronomist who planted them was Dr. M.S. Swaminathan at the Indian Agricultural Research Institute in New Delhi.

Peering through his big black glasses, Dr. Swaminathan watched with interest as the short wheats sprouted and grew. Intrigued by the stumpy stalks, he examined the plants daily. The seed heads swelled and he counted twice as much grain on one plant than on Indian varieties. Could this wheat save his country? To find out, Dr. Swaminathan invited Norm to India.

In March of 1963, Norm arrived in New Delhi. Dr. Swaminathan greeted him with warmth, and right away Norm knew they would become good friends. The two agronomists toured India's major wheat-growing areas along the Ganges River. They also traveled up into the Himalayan foothills where the temperatures dropped to near freezing at night. As Dr. Swaminathan shivered, Norm pulled out his old purple wrestling singlet—which he always kept in his suitcase!— and put it on underneath his clothes. Years later, Dr. Swaminathan remembered that Norm was the only one who managed to stay warm at night.

Throughout his travels, Norm couldn't help comparing India's northern region with Mexico's Yaqui Valley. Both sat at the same latitude and had similar climates. In the Yaqui Valley, farmers harvested 6,000 pounds of wheat per acre. In India, farmers were lucky to get 700–800 pounds. Norm became convinced India could make the same transformation Mexico had.

Dr. Swaminathan asked Norm if the dwarf wheat would help India. Norm didn't like to offer false hope. Give me a few weeks, he said, and I will write you a report. Norm first had to see if his trainees from Pakistan and Egypt had been successful with their dwarf wheat.

Hidden Hope

From India, Norm traveled to Pakistan where he met Nur Chaudry and Mansur Bajwa, his Pakistani trainees. They introduced him to the head of the Agricultural Research Institute who led the group out to the field. The official boasted about the tall wonder of Pakistani wheat. Norm wanted to see his semi-dwarf wheat, hoping it would be growing well even though it was halfway around the world from where it was created. The administrator pointed to a small row a few feet away.

Oh no! Norm's semi-dwarfs drooped like soggy socks. Clearly the trainees hadn't cared for them properly. Why didn't they plant it appropriately? Why didn't they fertilize? Norm demanded answers.

Chaudry and Bajwa were silent as their boss explained to Norm: Only a certain amount of fertilizer was allowed and Norm's recommendations were too high. Norm suspected his trainees' experiments had been sabotaged by the senior official who didn't want to admit his country needed outside help.

Before sunrise the next day, Norm woke to a tap, tap, tap on his window. Chaudry and Bajwa motioned for Norm to join them. The three men hurried single-file through the wheat field. In a far corner, Chaudry and Bajwa stopped and stepped aside so Norm could see.

Even in the dim light, Norm recognized his wheat just as well as he would Jeanie or Bill. Each stiff stalk was shooting up from the ground proudly holding heavy heads of grain. The trainees had secretly planted a second plot so the head of the institute wouldn't see it. "I could have danced," Norm said. "I took a closer look at that little green patch and knew in a moment we had something on our hands for Pakistan—and for India."[78] Norm thanked them for risking their careers by going against the institute's wishes.

Norm was so excited he could have flown to Egypt on his own enthusiasm. Seeing his wheats growing well in Pakistan confirmed his belief he'd created a wheat for the whole world—a wheat that could curb Hunger. But would he find the same results in Egypt?

REBEL

"I am not one to sit idly by .... If I have anything to contribute to this world, I'm going to play that card and play it hard."[79]

From Pakistan, Norm flew to Egypt. It was his fiftieth birthday. There, he discovered his trainees had been forced to hide their wheat experiment too. Far from the skeptical glare of their director, Norm cheered at the secret sight. Healthy, semi-dwarf wheat growing on the other side of the planet was the best birthday present ever.

Convinced beyond a doubt the semi-dwarf wheat could revitalize Pakistan and India, Norm launched a plan. The first nation to welcome his help was Pakistan. President Ayub Khan no longer wanted to take food aid from foreign countries. He was so enthusiastic about semi-dwarf wheat, he started a patch of it in the garden at the presidential residence. India would take longer to win over, but Norm's strategy was the same—he had to convince conservative politicians, overcome agricultural scientists' fear, and earn the farmers' trust.

Norm's political connections in Pakistan included President Ayub Kahn and the Agricultural Minister Malik Khuda Bucha Bakhsh. Norm asked Nacho to work with scientists and set up test plots in farmers' fields. In India, Shari C. Subramanian, the agricultural minister, represented the government's interests. Dr. M.S. Swaminathan would oversee the science, and Dr. Glenn Anderson, a Canadian agronomist, would organize test plots.

Norm's strategy had three parts: technology, psychology, and economics. Norm had already taken care of the technology, wrestling for two decades with wheat plants to create his rust-resistant, high-yielding, semi-dwarf variety. He also established protocols for how to prepare the fields, sow the seeds, deal with weeds, fertilize, and harvest.

Psych Out

In Pakistan, Nacho and his team planted experimental plots at the major agricultural schools and at several farms across the wheat-growing region. The first harvest averaged three tons, which crushed the measly 0.8 tons Pakistani farmers had previously produced, and showed what a difference the new seed could make in their lives.

Now, Norm sought to rally support from skeptical agricultural scientists. He expected a casual meet and greet with a few researchers, but when he entered the meeting room at the Pakistani Department of Agriculture, he faced a committee of stone-faced professors. Norm steeled himself for attack.

The first scientist to speak waved a fist full of papers. Anyone who predicts that the wheat crop will double in eight years must be insane, he said, criticizing Norm's research and belittling the idea Mexican wheat could ever grow in Pakistan. They threw out all sorts of excuses: their farmers were illiterate and didn't like change, the dwarf wheat would starve their buffalos, it would poison their women. One professor even accused Norm of being a CIA spy!

Then it was Norm's turn to speak.

Norm refuted each and every statement. Choosing his words carefully, he explained how eager the Pakistani farmers were to better their lives. The semi-dwarf wheat produced more than enough straw to feed Pakistan's buffalo. In all his years, his wheat had never poisoned a single person, and no, he was not with the CIA. There was one complaint the agriculturalist stubbornly clung to. The committee insisted that Pakistani people would never grow or eat red wheat.

Norm explained that the light pink color of Lerma Rojo was on the husk only and did not affect the color of the grain inside. He assured them the Mexican grain was as white as traditional Pakistani wheat.

The authorities were not convinced.

There was only way to solve the conflict. The agricultural minister asked his kitchen staff to bake two batches of traditional Pakistani bread called naan—one from flour ground from local wheat and one from flour ground from Norm's Mexican wheat.

The grumpy critics put on blindfolds, then smelled and tasted the naan.

The breads smelled the same. The breads tasted the same. No one could tell the difference. Satisfied, Norm left before they could invent another excuse.

Cargo Chaos

President Ayub Khan ordered 250 tons of Norm's seed from Mexico, and promised to provide fertilizer to Pakistani farmers. Norm casually mentioned this development to Indian officials. The two countries had always been rivals and he hoped to spark a reaction. His plan worked. Not wanting to be left behind, India ordered 200 tons of seed. Now the problem was, how were Norm and his team going to ship these huge orders of seed halfway around the world in time for planting? It had never been done before.

Working backward, Norm figured out a timeline. The seed had to be in the ground by the middle of November. It would take a month to distribute the seed to all the farmers. That put it back to mid-October. Mexico did not export seed, so the order would have to be shipped from the United States. A cargo ship took about six weeks to travel from the Port of Los Angeles to India, and another week to get to Pakistan. That put it back to mid-August. And it was already August! There was no time to lose. A ship was leaving on August 12, and the seed for India and for Pakistan had to be aboard.

On August 7, 1965, with Nacho in the lead, thirty loaded semi-trucks headed to the Mexico/U.S. border. Customs refused to let them cross. For four days, Nacho argued with border officials. Finally, on August 11, the trucks motored north to Los Angeles. In Mexico, Norm was waiting for news, but no call came. The seeds had less than a day to leave port. What was happening?

On August 13, Norm's phone rang, but it wasn't Nacho. There was a misspelling in the Indian paperwork; new contracts had to be prepared. But that would take days! There were no computers or scanners to speed up the process.

As the convoy of trucks neared Los Angeles on Saturday, August 14, Nacho saw black smoke billowing across the sky. All traffic stopped. A riot was raging in the Los Angeles neighborhood of Watts. Police, FBI, and the National Guard had barricaded the area. They would not let the life-saving cargo pass no matter how much Nacho pleaded.

Finally, on Sunday night, authorities allowed the trucks to roll. Burnt-out cars smoldered. Glass littered the ground where windows had been shattered. Thirty-four people had been killed in the Civil Rights riots.

At the docks, the authorities refused to load the seed without the corrected paperwork. Nacho called Norm. Maybe if it had been any other problem, Norm would have waited the extra day or two until everything was legal. But this hold-up involved PAPERWORK!

Norm thought of the million dollars–worth of seed sitting on the pier. He thought about the millions of Hungry people who would starve without this wheat. It was like the penny sales during the depression—sometimes the right thing to do was not always the lawful thing to do.

"Put the seed on the ship," he ordered Nacho. "I'll take the responsibility, and if something goes wrong, by God I'll personally pay it off myself ... if it takes the rest of my life!"[80]

The shipment of seed sailed on Monday, August 16. It was late, but for the first time in a long time, Norm felt relaxed enough to sit with Margaret and listen to the radio.

War Zone

The 1965 war between India and Pakistan began August 5 when Indian tanks crossed the border into Pakistan. Each country claimed ownership of the region of Kashmir. Fighting lasted seventeen days, but fits of firing continued to occur all across the border area near several experimental fields.

He tuned in to a news report. War had broken out between India and Pakistan. That was one problem that even Norm couldn't fix. But he could prevent one country from withholding seed from the other. Quickly, Norm called the shipping line. India's seed was put on one boat, and Pakistan's order was placed on another.

In early December, Nacho called Norm. All the seed was in the ground! Norm was delighted. "This huge and complex operation of seeding an area amounting to 12,000 acres scattered across the country would have been hard enough without a war going on," he said. "However, despite all the trans-shipments ... ninety-nine percent of the seed got to the right place and was planted properly."[81]

Wheat Fever

By 1967, many irrigated fields across India were growing lush and green with semi-dwarf wheat. Just like the Mexican *campesinos,* the farmers in India had to see the improvements for themselves, and it wasn't enough to show a 15 percent increase in grain. It had to be spectacular—100 percent, 200 percent—and it was.

Seeing one farmer succeed fueled other farmers to hurry their own prosperity. Desperate for Norm's "miracle" seed, some farmers raided test plots. The Indian Agricultural Research Institute posted armed guards to prevent the seed from being stolen. It didn't always work. Researchers found one guard tied, naked, to a tree. All the heads of the wheat had been snipped off.

The Field Days organized by Norm's Indian team attracted enormous crowds. Farmers came by the truckloads and stood in line all day to receive their allotment of seed. Professors planted wheat in their backyards, and students earned tuition money by selling seed.

As Norm toured the wheat region, farmers and their families ran to catch a glimpse of him or to touch his hand. The boldest farmers beckoned Norm to see their healthy crops. Others were close behind eager to show off too. Sometimes there were so many people vying for Norm's attention, his translator could barely keep up. These were the real heroes in Norm's eyes. They had had the courage to change, and change could lead to prosperity.

Unfortunately, not all Indian farmers prospered.

Famine

From 1966 through 1967, the northern region of India was suffering from a severe drought. The seasonal monsoon winds that usually brought life-giving rains failed to show. March was the time when farmers should have been cutting their crops. Children *should have been* giggling and gathering the sheaves. Women *should have been* beating the sheaves to free the grain. Others *should have been* winnowing the grain, letting the feather-light husks fly away. But the fields in Northern India were silent during the spring of 1967. The grain bins sat empty. For the first time since 1947, India declared an official famine. Across 20,000 square miles, more than 13 million people struggled to survive.

Most rural villages had no available drinking water. Women and children had to walk miles to the nearest working wells. Where once people poled their boats down the River Tilaiya, they resorted to riding their bicycles along the dry, cracked river bed.

The Indian government set up relief programs. Food-for-Work projects gave those who were able to work a way to earn food rations and keep their dignity. Emaciated men broke rock with sledge hammers, dug wells, or built houses.

For the first time, American families saw images on nightly news programs of frail, worried women holding starving babies. Aid from the United States, Canada, and other countries couldn't get to the starving people fast enough. Sacks of grain piled up at Indian railroad stations because there weren't enough railroad cars or men to distribute the food.

In cities throughout India, students rioted and threw stones at government buildings, demanding action. The sounds reverberating through the streets reminded Norm of that milk strike so many years ago. Walking through Bombay (now Mumbai), Norm saw homeless children hovering around hotels, pleading for scraps of bread, for food of any kind. "Each morning trucks circled the streets, picking up corpses," Norm said. "That's when my patience ran out. I knew how to intensify every acre's production of wheat. And I knew there was no time to lose."[82]

Wrestling with Bureaucracy

In order to feed ALL of India, Norm needed to secure the economic part of his plan. It wasn't enough to have scientists embrace Norm's technology, or to have farmers waiting hungrily to double or triple their yield, without government assistance Norm's plan would fail. The farmers needed access to credit to purchase seed and fertilizer and the guarantee of fair prices at market so they could pay off loans and make a profit. Unfortunately, one of Norm's biggest advocates, the minister of agriculture, had lost his re-election. Now Norm had to grapple with Deputy Prime Minister Ashok Mehta, who controlled policy-making. Mehta believed in funding industry, not agriculture.

Walking into the minister's office felt like walking into a wrestling ring with a much larger opponent. Norm made the first move, outlining how the deputy prime minister could help the starving people in the Bihar region. Give farmers credit to purchase fertilizer! Guarantee a fair price for the farmer's crop!

Although he was scoring points, Norm could not pin Mehta to the mat, but he would not give up. "Unless such a change in policy is forthcoming soon," he said, "the enthusiasm and expectations of hundreds of thousands of farmers will change to frustration and give rise to social and political disorder." He leaned in. "If this happens ... you will be ousted!"[83]

Mehta leaped to his feet. How dare Norm give *him* orders. For several minutes the two men shouted at each other. It was a miracle no military guards came to take Norm away.

Exhausted, the adversaries fell back into their chairs, glaring at each other.

Norm broke the silence with an apology. Then he said, "Multiply everything for farm support three to four times. Then you will be closer to what is needed to keep India from starving."[84]

As Norm prepared to leave the room, he made his last move. In exasperation he shouted, "IMAGINE YOUR COUNTRY FREE OF FAMINE. IT IS WITHIN YOUR GRASP!"[85]

That night Norm flew home to Mexico, wondering who had won

the bout. Was this the last time he'd be allowed into India? Would anyone else continue to fight? Hunger could not win.

On April 1, 1967, Indian newspapers announced a change in policy. Deputy Prime Minister Mehta promised to negotiate with companies to build fertilizer factories and to give farmers access to credit. Finally!

Years later when asked what his toughest wrestling match was, Norm said it was that shouting match with the deputy prime minister of India.

Feast

Norm's multi-pronged approach to give farmers the semi-dwarf seed, access to fertilizer, and support from the government turned the 1968 Indian harvest into one of the busiest in history. Typically, harvest took three weeks to bring in 800 pounds of grain per acre. That year, farmers worked non-stop for two months hauling in 3,000 to 7,000 pounds per acre. Farmers and their families labored day and night cutting stalks and stacking sheaves. In some areas there weren't enough people to do all the work.

When farmers brought wheat into towns to be processed, there were too few threshing floors. Bullocks worked overtime trampling in circles, each footstep knocking the grain free from the stalks. The country ran out of cloth sacks and tasked prisoners to sew more. Towns ran out of storage facilities. They cancelled school so classrooms could be filled with wheat.

The semi-dwarf wheat that had been planted on only 18 percent of the land, accounted for 36 percent of the seventeen-million-ton harvest. In four short years between 1964 and 1968, more wheat was grown than in the previous 4,000 years!

In July 1968, Prime Minister Indira Gandhi released a postage stamp to commemorate India's "Wheat Revolution 1968." It featured three heads of wheat and the library building of the Indian Agricultural Research Institute. A year later, William Gaud from the United States Agency for International Development labeled the incredible rise in grain production as the "Green Revolution." The name stuck.

India went on to build more fertilizer factories and tractor plants. They created the largest national wheat research program in the world, and were well on their way to being self-sufficient in wheat.

Besides more wheat, there was also more optimism. Indian scientists, once afraid to think big, now sought future discoveries, and government officials learned to support new ideas. Farmers finally earned the respect they deserved as food providers for their entire nation. People cheered the slogan, *Jai Jawan, Jai Kisan,* "Hail the Soldier, Hail the Farmer," elevating farmers to soldiers battling Hunger.

With more confidence and capital, farmers experimented with three-season planting, dug more wells, and invested in their families. Villages were coming to life with newly built houses and roads. Norm's semi-dwarf seed grew more than just wheat. It filled farmers'

wallets and fueled industry. It sparked international scientific cooperation and a global awareness of food insecurity.

Emergency!

In 1969, on one of Norm's last visits to Lahore, Pakistan, he was pulled aside by a man with a concerned look on his face. He said a nearby farm had a field of Norm's wheat, but something was wrong. It was sick.

Norm's stomach tightened. Could it be an attack of a new kind of rust? If that were the case, the entire country's wheat supply was in imminent danger. Norm hurried into the man's van and they sped off. So far he'd been successful tackling every problem thrown his way, but, Norm wondered, what if this was a problem he could not solve?

HUMBLE HEART

"If you desire peace, cultivate justice, but at the same time cultivate the fields to produce more bread; otherwise there will be no peace."[86]

The trip to the "nearby" farm took over an hour. The sun dipped below the horizon as they pulled up to a large field which, even in the dim light, Norm could tell was healthy. "It was still deep green in color and so dense, uniform and plump and sturdy that one could toss his hat onto the flat surface of the plump heads and there it would stay."[87]

The nervous farmer met them, gesturing for Norm to follow. They trekked to an open area; still Norm could see no sign of shriveled leaves or wilted stalks, or smell a rotten odor. What was going on?

Lights flickered behind them. Frustrated, Norm turned to go back to the van, but what he saw stopped him in his tracks. Several lanterns illuminated a group of smiling villagers.

"Dr. Borlaug," said the farmer, "we apologize for bringing you here under false pretenses, but we wanted somehow to thank you for changing our lives. This new wheat will make it possible for me to get married…. We will build a house where we now stand. We knew not how to show our appreciation. So, we asked the women. They went to work and made this."

Two women stepped forward to present Norm with a beautiful quilt. Every family in the village had created a quilt square. "Take this home to Mrs. Borlaug, please. Keep it as a reminder that without the new wheat, the better life we see ahead would not have been possible."[88]

Norm was moved beyond words. This was the greatest gift he'd ever received.

Margaret Insists

One year later, on October 20, 1970, Norm struggled to make sense of what Margaret was saying as they stood on opposite sides of the irrigation ditch. He'd just won the Nobel Peace Prize, she said. The phone hadn't stopped ringing. Reporters from around the world wanted to know what he thought about the honor. If this was all true, Norm's quiet life in the field was over.

Margaret urged Norm to come see for himself.

No. He had work to do. He waved Margaret back to the car and returned to his students.

Less than an hour later, a van drove up and a television crew piled out with their equipment. "Which one of you guys is Borlaug?"[89]

Norm tried to shoo them away, but when more press arrived, he gave up and stood before the cameras, sweat-stained, dirty, and totally flummoxed. "The Nobel Prize hit me like a typhoon," he said later.[90] "It threw me into the spotlight so much it made me uncomfortable." He eventually needed to hire a secretary to help him keep up with all the paperwork

Unconventional Hero

That December, Norm, Margaret, Jeanie, and Bill flew to Oslo, Norway, for the Nobel Peace Prize ceremony. There they met King Olaf and visited the village where Norm's great-grandparents Ole and Solveig Borlaug once lived.

On December 10, 1970, before a sparkly audience, Mrs. Aase Lionaes, chair of the Peace Prize committee, introduced Norm. "He has devoted all his energy to achieving the historical result which today is referred to all over the world as the "green revolution." This revolution will make it possible to improve the living conditions of hundreds of millions of people…. Behind the outstanding results in the sphere of wheat ... we sense the presence of a dynamic, indomitable, and refreshingly unconventional research scientist."[91]

Norm looked dashing in his tuxedo. There was not one speck of dirt under his fingernails. Norm looked out at the audience, to his family—Margaret, Jeanie, and Bill—who had never complained about his long absences, and to his friends from Mexico who took a chance and trusted the blue-eyed *gringo*. He thought about his *agronomos*, hundreds of them from all over the world, and everyone else he worked with over thirty years. This prize, he said, "belonged to an army of hunger fighters."[92]

A New Normal

Norm's life was never the same after that. Thrust into the spotlight, he shouldered the extra responsibility of being the face and voice of the Green Revolution. Although he preferred the peace of a wheat field, Norm accepted as many invitations as he could to lecture and inform

The Nobel Peace Prize

This prize is awarded to the person who, during the preceding year, contributed the most to benefit humankind. Alfred Nobel, for whom the prize is named, created this honor to encourage others to strive for goodness. The first Peace Prize was awarded in 1901. Nobel once said, "I would rather take care of the stomachs of the living than the glory of the departed in the form of monuments." Norm was the first, and so far only, agriculturalist to receive the award.

the public about the ongoing battle against Hunger. He continued to work at CIMMYT and inspire young agronomists. But he also grappled with critics who felt that agricultural science was harmful

---

"

"I am acutely conscious of the fact that I am but one member of that vast army and so I want to share not only the present honor but also the future obligations with all my companions in arms, for the Green Revolution has not yet been won."[93]

---

to the environment. No one loved the natural world more than Norm, but he could never turn his back on hungry children. He'd witnessed too many of them die of starvation. Norm often thought that if the critics "... experienced the physical sensation of hunger. If they lived just one month amid the misery of the developing world, as I have for fifty years, they'd be crying out for tractors and fertilizer and irrigation canals."[94]

In 1984, Norm joined the faculty of Texas A&M University, adding classroom teaching to his illustrious career. For the first time in many years, he and Margaret lived in the United States, in College Station, Texas. From there he traveled around the world wherever food scarcity threatened humanity.

In 1986, Norm joined forces with philanthropist Ryoichi Sasakawa and U.S. President Jimmy Carter to improve agriculture in fifteen sub-Saharan African countries. Norm helped more than eight million small-scale farmers feed their families. Even at the age of 90, when a new deadly strain of stem rust appeared in Uganda, Norm jumped into action. The Bill and Melinda Gates Foundation heeded his warnings and helped create the Borlaug Global Rust Initiative (BGRI), which has grown into an international consortium of more than 1,000 scientists from hundreds of institutions to battle the global threats to wheat security.

"No one loves wildlife more than I do—no one. But I also love man and I want to see his children fed."[95]

World Food Prize

Winning the Nobel Peace Prize made Norm think about the importance of acknowledging all the people who worked tirelessly to end Hunger. In 1986, Norm created the World Food Prize (WFP) to honor "the achievements of individuals who have advanced human development by improving the quality, quantity, or availability of food in the world."[96] The recipient of the first World Food Prize was Norm's friend and Indian agronomist Dr. M.S. Swaminathan.

Smylie's Prediction

In Norm's high school yearbook, his friend Robert Smylie predicted Norm would win the "Congressional Award for Valor." Smylie was *almost* right. There is no medal for valor, but in 2007, Congress awarded Norm the Congressional Gold Medal. Norm also received the Presidential Medal of Freedom (1977), making him one of only five people to have ever received the three highest international honors: the Nobel Peace Prize, the Congressional Gold Medal, and the Medal of Freedom. The four other people who've received all three honors are Martin Luther King, Jr., Mother Teresa, Elie Weisel, and Nelson Mandela.

The WFP honors thinkers and doers—people who have created organizations such as Heifer International and Bread for the World, as well as those who have developed freshwater fish farming, innovated micro-irrigation, and created new ways to transport vegetables. It has gone to people who work directly with crops, impoverished communities, and policy makers.

Norm also created the WFP Youth Institute because he not only saw potential in a tiny seed, he saw potential in young people, and like Reyes and the other bird boys, the teens of the future will one day be in charge. The Youth Institute encourages young people to think about poverty and Hunger in their own communities and across the globe. Students from around the world research a food scarcity problem and present a solution. Chosen teens are invited to present their ideas to an audience of professors, agricultural experts, and other students. At the WFP, everyone's ideas are treated with the same respect because, as Norm knew, anyone's idea could be the spark for the next Green Revolution.

Our Loss

On September 12, 2009, Norm died peacefully in his Texas home at the age of ninety-five. All across the globe, millions of people mourned. Many of them owed their very lives to Norm's innovations.

Remarkably, in many countries where food is plentiful, millions of people had no idea who Norman Borlaug was or why his death made the headlines. They didn't realize they too benefited from Norm's lifelong efforts. Much of the bread eaten around the world is made from the descendants of Norm's semi-dwarf varieties, and his shuttle-breeding method is still used by breeders today. But he wouldn't have cared if people knew his name, as long as they no longer knew Hunger.

It is this contrast of fame and obscurity that characterized Norm's life. He was bold enough to tackle world-jarring problems, yet he battled peacefully in a Mexican wheat field. He had the confidence to stand up to world leaders, yet he had the compassion to work beside the poorest farmers.

Norm learned his childhood lessons well. He wasn't afraid, he gave it his all, and he never quit. He never did become the second baseman for the Chicago Cubs, but he was the star player on a much

more important international team of Hunger fighters. He didn't become a wrestling coach either, but he did inspire thousands of young men and women to grapple with world Hunger.

Not long before he died, a friend asked Norm if he had any regrets. Norm was silent for a time. Then, with a tear in his eye, he said. "That I haven't done enough."[97]

How remarkable coming from a man who fed the world.

A Call to Action

"
"Hunger still exists in places Norm couldn't reach, and we all owe it to him to remove the threat of famine once and for all."[98]

— U.S. PRESIDENT JIMMY CARTER

More than Just Wheat

Norm may have started the Green Revolution, but the drastic increase in grain yield involved more than just wheat. Researchers in the Philippines used some of Norm's techniques and produced a variety of rice that yielded five times more than older varieties. Countries other than India and Pakistan also benefited. Afghanistan, Sri Lanka, China, Indonesia, Iran, Kenya, Malaya, Morocco, Thailand, Tunisia, and Turkey experienced their own Green Revolutions by adopting Norm's ideas of using high-yielding crops, fertilizers, and other technology like pest control, irrigation, and mechanization.

The Next Norm

Norm and Hunger circled each other like wrestlers on a mat for nearly seventy years. Sadly, his work is not yet finished. Today there are more than seven billion humans on the planet, of which about one billion live in poverty and experience Hunger every day. In the United States alone, one in seven people experience "food insecurity," which means they don't have the money for access to enough healthy nutritious food. How do we bring that number to zero?

It will take a group effort of dedicated farmers, innovative scientists, empathetic policy-makers, and YOU. Part of the solution depends on the choices you, your family, and your friends make every day.

Here are a few good choices to start with.

CHOOSE TO:

Waste less — Every day, the average American throws away one pound of food. That adds up to 40 percent of our food supply each year. That's food which could have fed someone else. And it's not just the food that's wasted, it's also the time, energy, and resources that went into growing that food. Every year, 25 percent of all irrigation water and a land area the size of Canada is used in producing food no one eats.

- Eat or cook that slightly bruised apple or banana rather than throwing it out.

- Take only what you know you will eat in the school cafeteria.

- Help your family plan meals. Create a menu, make a grocery list, and buy only what you need for those meals.

- Learn how to store food properly so it doesn't spoil.

Donate to food pantries — Food pantries provide much needed food for those who may not be able to purchase all of their groceries. Locate the food pantries near you. Find out what foods they need most. Volunteer your time to stock shelves or fill bags.

Eat local — This movement encourages people to eat food grown near you. Even if you live in a city, there are still farms all around you. Visit a farmer's market and meet local farmers. Eating local supports those farms, and saves on the cost of transporting produce.

Participate in the World Food Prize Youth Institute — Check out the Youth Institute's website: www.worldfoodprize.org/en/youth_ programs/youth_institutes/. Participate in the essay contest. It's a great way to learn about food scarcity and get a feel for the kinds of careers available in agriculture and other related fields.

Celebrate World Food Day on October 16 — Visit the Food & Agriculture Organization for ways to celebrate: www.fao.org/world-food-day/take-action/en/

Get involved — You will soon be living in a world with nine billion people—the most ever! It will take a lot of work to make sure no one goes hungry. Become a hero for the hungry today.

95
Years of
Norm

1914 – born March 25 in Saude, Iowa

1932 – graduates Cresco High School

1933 – enrolls at University of Minnesota

1937 – marries Margaret Gibson

1942 – works at Dupont

1944 – joins Mexico's Agricultural Program;
battles rust in Mexico

1946 – develops shuttle breeding

1953 – begins research on dwarf wheat

1956 – Mexico self-sufficient in grain

1960 – training program goes international

1968 – Pakistan self-sufficient in wheat

1970 – wins Nobel Peace Prize

1972 – India self-sufficient in wheat

1977 – receives Presidential Medal of Freedom

1984 – joins Texas A & M;
famine in African countries

1986 – creates World Food Prize

1999 – battles rust in Uganda

2001 – battles rust in Kenya

2003 – battles rust in Ethiopia

2007 – awarded Congressional Gold Medal

2009 – dies September 21 at the age of 95

> ❝
> You've got to reach for the star.
> You'll never get the star ... but if you stretch yourself
> enough ... you'll get some stardust on your hands.
> And if that happens, you'll be surprised with ... your
> ability to do something for yourself, your family, the
> community, the state, the nation, and the world."[99]

Learn More About Norman Borlaug

- University of Minnesota, College of Food, Agricultural and Natural Resource Sciences, "Norman Borlaug" at borlaug.cfans.umn.edu/

- Texas A&M University, "Borlaug Archives" at borlaugarchives.tamu.edu/digital-archives/

- Norman Borlaug Heritage Foundation at normanborlaug.org

- World Food Prize, "About Norman Borlaug" at worldfoodprize.org/youth_programs_map/

- Nobel Prize, "Norman Borlaug" at nobelprize.org/prizes/peace/1970/borlaug/facts/

• Source Notes •

"1960's: India's Changing Phase." *India Today*, 14 Aug. 2013, www.indiatoday.in/magazine/india-today-archives/story/20070702-indian-decade-of-dos and donts-1960s-748418-1999-11-30.

Belair, Felix, Jr. "Farming Revolution in Poorer Lands Is Held Near." *The New York Times,* Special Ed. 8, 14 May 1968.

Bickel, Lennard. *Facing Starvation: Norman Borlaug and the Fight Against Hunger.* New York: Reader's Digest Press, 1974.

Borlaug, Norman, E. "Acceptance speech on the occasion of the award of the Nobel Peace Prize." Nobel Institute, Oslo, Norway, 10 Dec. 1970.

———. "Afterword." Noel Vietmeyer. *Borlaug: Bread Winner.* Lorton, Virginia: Bracing Books, 2004.

———. "The Green Revolution, Peace, and Humanity." Nobel Lecture, Nobel Institute, Oslo, Norway, 11 Dec. 1970.

———. Interviewed by Paul Underwood, Dec. 2005. "Norman Borlaug: Henry Wallace and the Beginnings of the Mexican Agricultural Program." 23:45 min, *Wessels Living History Farm,* Ganzel Group of Communications, 2007, livinghistoryfarm.org/podcasts/BorlaugMexico.m4v.

———. Interviewed by Paul Underwood, Dec. 2005. "Norman Borlaug: On Growing Up on an Iowa Farm." 27:28 min, *Wessels Living History Farm,* Ganzel Group of Communications, 2007, livinghistoryfarm.org/podcasts/BorlaugBio.m4v.

———. Interviewed by Paul Underwood, Dec. 2005. "Norman Borlaug: On the Four Factors Affecting Agriculture in Food Deficit Nations." 23:53 min, Wessels Living History Farm, Ganzel Group of Communications, 2007, livinghistoryfarm.org/farminginthe50s/movies/borlaug_crops_16.html?%20iframe=true&%20width=%20105%%20&height=%20105%.

———. "Nobel Centennial Symposium." 6 Dec. 2001, Oslo, Norway. www.nobelprize.org/mediaplayer/?id=1162.

———. "Sixty-two Years of Fighting Hunger: Personal Recollections" *Euphytica,* Springer Science & Business Media. B.V. 2007, The Borlaug Archives, TAMU, it-lfecmweb.tamu.edu/borlaugwl/0/doc/50869/Page1.aspx.

———. "1980 Interview with Dr. Norman Borlaug: Life, Population, and Food." 33:58 min, CIMMYT, 2009. Internet Archive: Digital Library, Our Media, 2001, archive.org/details/CIMMYT1980InterviewwithDr.NormanBorlaugaboutaspectsoflife_populationandfood.

———. "1987 Interview with Norman Borlaug: His and CIMMYT'S History." 59:01 min, CIMMYT, youtu.be/_Fm48yzlH1I.

Borlaug, Norman, E., and Anwar S. Dil. *Norman Borlaug on World Hunger.* Intercultural Forum, 1997.

"Breadbasket Diplomacy." *Time,* 2 Dec. 1965, p. 25.

Carter, Jimmy. "Take it to the Farmer." Speech given at Sasakawa Africa Association's 2010 Borlaug Symposium, Carter Center, 2010, www.cartercenter.org/news/editorials_speeches/borlaug-tribute-saa2010.html.

"Celebrating 100 Years of Dr. Norman Borlaug, 25 March 2014." 3:06 min, CIMMYT, youtu.be/FRwo01maYqY.

"Dr. Norman Borlaug: Stars," *AgriLifeVideo,* Texas A&M, 1997, youtu.be/nACAyqoWScY?list=PL93EA3145F56ADD86.

Easterbrook, Gregg. "Forgotten Benefactor of Humanity." *The Atlantic,* January 1997, www.theatlantic.com/magazine/archive/1997/01/forgotten-benefactor-of-humanity/306101/.

"Feeding 10 Billion by 2050." The Forum at Harvard T. H. Chan School of Public Health, 28 May 2019, theforum.sph.harvard.edu/events/feeding-10-billion-by-2050/.

Fletcher Stoeltje, Melissa. "The Man Who Feeds Millions." *Texas,* 7 Dec. 1997, p. 8, umedia.lib.umn.edu/item/p16022coll345:5343/p16022coll345:5257?child_index=4&query=&sidebar_page=2.

"Freedom from Famine: The Norman Borlaug Story" 56:46 min, Philip Courter, Mathile Institute, 2009, vimeo.com/136654007.

Gillis, Justin. "Norman Borlaug, Father of a Crop Revolution, Dies at 95." *The New York Times—Breaking News, World News & Multimedia,* 13 Sept. 2009, www.nytimes.com/2009/09/14/business/energy-environment/14borlaug.html.

Global Reach Internet Productions, LLC—Ames, IA—globalreach.com. "The World Food Prize—Improving the Quality, Quantity and Availability of Food in the World," www.worldfoodprize.org/.

———. "About Norman Borlaug." The World Food Prize, www.worldfoodprize.org/en/dr_norman_e_borlaug/about_norman_borlaug/.

Davidson, Mary Gray. "An Abundant Harvest: Interview with Norman Borlaug, Recipient, Nobel Peace Prize, 1970." *AgBioWorld,* 12 Aug. 1997, www.agbioworld.org/biotech-info/topics/borlaug/abundant.html.

"The Green Revolution & Dr Norman Borlaug: Towards the "Evergreen Revolution." *AgBioWorld,* www.agbioworld.org/biotech-info/topics/borlaug/green-revolution.html.

Hesser, Leon. *Man Who Fed the World.* Dallas, Texas: Durban House Press, Inc., 2009.

Honan, Kim. "Inside the world's largest wheat and maize bank." *ABC Rural,* 14 Apr. 2014, www.abc.net.au/news/rural/2014-04-15/largest-wheat-and-seed-collection-in-world/5384518.

"India: The Threat of Famine." *Time,* 2 Dec. 1965, p. 36.

Kautzky, Keagan, Educational Program Director. Interview via Zoom, 8 May 2019, 1:00pm.

Lionaes, Aase. "Nobel Peace Prize Presentation Speech" Oslo, Norway, 1970, www.nobelprize.org/prizes/peace/1970/ceremony-speech/.

"The Man Who Saved a Billion Lives." *SeedWorld,* 15 Jan. 2015, seedworld.com/man-saved-billion-lives/.

Mann, Charles C. *The Wizard and the Prophet: Two Remarkable Scientists and Their Dueling Visions to Shape Tomorrow's World.* New York: Alfred A. Knopf, 2018.

Nevard, Jacques. "Hunger Grows in India." *The New York Times,* 1 Aug. 1960.

"Norman Borlaug: A Billion Lives Saved." *AgBioWorld,* www.agbioworld.org/biotech-info/topics/borlaug/special.html.

"Norman Borlaug: Interview with Peter Jennings." 4:46 min, *World News Tonight,* ABC 2004, youtu.be/A879aLW9B_g.

"Norman Borlaug: Nobel Peace Prize 1970." 00:58 min, Oslo, Norway, 6 Dec. 2001.

"Peace Prize to Wheat Breeder." Indian Miller, Sept. 1970, Vol. 1, No. 2, Borlaug Papers, University of Minnesota.

Phillips, Ronald L. "Norman E. Borlaug Biographical Memoir." National Academy of Sciences, 2013, www.nasonline.org/publications/biographical-memoirs/memoir-pdfs/borlaug-norman.pdf.

Schob, David. "Iowa Farming during 1910-1920 as seen through the eyes of Paul Corey's Mantz Trilogy."

"The Story of Norman Borlaug, the American Scientist Who Helped Engineer India's Green Revolution." *The Better India,* 2 May 2017, www.thebetterindia.com/98602/norman-borlaug-america-india-green-revolution/.

Streeter, Carroll P. "The Wheat Breeder Who Won the Peace Prize." *Farm Journal,* Dec. 1970, pp. 16–29, umedia.lib.umn.edu/item/p16022coll345:8271.

Swaminathan, M.S. "The Green Revolution." *50 Years of Green Revolution,* 2017, pp. 33–36.

Swanson, Lora. *Norman Borlaug: Hero in a Hurry.* BookSurge, 2009.

Vietmeyer, Noel. *Borlaug: Right off the Farm 1914-1944*. Lorton, Virginia: Bracing Books, 2009.

———. *Borlaug: Wheat Whisperer 1944-1959*. Lorton, Virginia: Bracing Books, 2011.

———. *Borlaug: Bread Winner 1960-1969*. Lorton, Virginia: Bracing Books, 2010.

World Food Prize. "Nomination Criteria" www.worldfoodprize.org/index.cfm?nodeID=87515&audienceID=1.

• Endnotes •

Chapter 1

1   Leon Hesser. *The Man Who Fed the World*. Dallas, Texas: Durban House Publishing, 2009, p. 1-3

2   Dr. Norman E. Borlaug, "Nobel Prize Lecture," Oslo, Norway, October 1970

3   Lennard Bickel. *Facing Starvation: Norman Borlaug and the Fight Against Hunger*. Reader's Digest Press, 1974, p.42

4   L. Hesser, p. 8

5   Vietmeyer, Noel. *Borlaug: Right off the Farm 1914-1944*. Lorton, Virginia: Bracing Books, 2009. vol. 1, p. 39

6   N. Vietmeyer, vol. 1, p. 39

7   N. Vietmeyer, vol. 1, p. 37

8   N. Vietmeyer, vol. 1, p. 48

9   N. Vietmeyer, vol. 1, p. 26

10   N. Vietmeyer, vol. 1, p. 54.

11   Charles C. Mann. *The Wizard and the Prophet: Two Remarkable Scientists and Their Dueling Visions to Shape Tomorrow's World*. New York: Alfred A. Knopf, 2018, p. 99

Chapter 2

12   Jack Jenkins. "Borlaug Comes Home." *The Farm Quarterly*, Jan – Feb 1971, p. 20

13   L. Hesser, p. 11

14   N. Vietmeyer, vol 1, p. 97

15   L. Hesser, p. 12

16   N. Vietmeyer, vol. 1, p. 104

17   N. Vietmeyer, vol. 1, p. 87

18   NEB's yearbook, *The Spartan*. 1932, p. 171

Chapter 3

19   L. Hesser, p. 15

20   "Dr. Norman Borlaug: Stars." *AgriLifeVideo*, Texas A & M, 1997

21   L. Hesser p. 16

22   N. Vietmeyer, vol. 1, p. 125

23   L. Hesser, p. 15

24   N. Vietmeyer, vol. 1, p. 126

25   N. Vietmeyer, vol. 1, p. 126

26   N. Vietmeyer, vol. 1, p. 129

27   N. Vietmeyer, vol. 1, p. 134

Chapter 4

28 N. Borlaug, "Afterword" for Vietmeyer vol. 3, p. 225
29 L. Bikel, p. 67
30 L. Bickel, p. 68
31 L. Hesser, p. 25
32 N. Vietmeyer, vol. 1, p. 204
33 L. Hesser, p. 25

Chapter 5

34 L. Bickel, p. 120
35 N. Vietmeyer, vol. 2, p. 25
36 N. Vietmeyer, vol. 2, p. 28
37 L. Hesser, p. 39
38 N. Vietmeyer, vol. 2, p. 206
39 "Peace Prize to Wheat Breeder." Indian Miller Sept. 1970, Vol. 1, No. 2. Borlaug Papers, University of Minnesota
40 "Peace Prize..." Indian Miller, 1970
41 L. Bickel, p. 137

Chapter 6

42 L. Bickel, p. 13
43 Vietmeyer, vol. 2, p. 47
44 N. Vietmeyer, vol. 2, p. 128
45 L. Hesser, p. 46
46 L. Hesser, p. 44
47 L. Hesser, p. 44
48 L. Bickel, p. 174

Chapter 7

49 L. Hesser, p. 50
50 N. Vietmeyer, vol. 2, p. 255
51 N. Vietmeyer, vol. 2, p. 42
52 N. Vietmeyer, vol. 2, p. 43
53 N. Vietmeyer, vol. 2, p. 71
54 N. Vietmeyer, vol. 2, p. 91
55 L. Hesser, p. 54
56 N. Vietmeyer, vol. 2, p. 131
57 N. Vietmeyer, vol. 2, p. 85
58 N. Vietmeyer, vol. 2, p. 143

Chapter 8

59   L. Bickel, p. 241
60   L. Bickel, p. 210
61   N. Borlaug letter to Paul Peterson, May 3, 2000.

Chapter 9

62   Phillips, Ronald L. "Norman E. Borlaug Biographical Memoir."
        National Academy of Sciences, 2013. p. 8.
63   San Bernardino Sun, March 6, 1958.
64   *The New York Times,* December 3, 1959
65   *The New York Times,* December 27, 1959
66   *The New York Times,* August 1, 1960
67   N. Vietmeyer, vol. 3, p.73
68   L. Bickel, p. 232
69   N. Borlaug, *Field Notebook,* 1963, p.10 University of Minnesota Libraries.
70   L. Bickel, p. 233
71   N. Vietmeyer, vol. 3, p. 26
72   N. Vietmeyer, vol. 3, 26
73   L. Bickel, p. 234
74   N. Vietmeyer, vol. 3, p. 32
75   "Freedom From Famine." 00:30. vimeo.com/136654007
76   "Peace Prize to Wheat Breeder." Indian Miller Sept. 1970, Vol. 1, No. 2.
        Borlaug Papers, University of Minnesota
77   Streeter, Carroll P. "The Wheat Breeder Who Won the Peace Prize." *Farm Journal,* Dec. 1970, p, 17, 29. umedia.lib.umn.edu/item/p16022coll345:8271.
78   L. Bickel, p. 248

Chapter 10

79   "Celebrating 100 Years of Dr. Norman Borlaug, 25 March 2014."
        CIMMYT, 2:25
80   N. Vietmeyer, vol. 3, p. 118
81   N. Vietmeyer, vol. 3, p. 120
82   N. Vietmeyer, vol. 3, p. 123
83   L. Hesser, p. 88
84   N. Vietmeyer, vol. 3, p. 169
85   V-3-169

Chapter 11

86   Borlaug, Nobel Lecture, 1970

87   N. Vietmeyer, vol. 3, p. 220

88   N. Vietmeyer, vol. 3, p. 221

89   L. Bickel, p. 341

90   L. Bickel, p. 341

91   A. Lionaes, "Nobel Peace Prize Presentation Speech," Oslo, Norway, 1970.

92   Borlaug, Nobel Acceptance Speech, 1970

93   Borlaug, Nobel Acceptance Speech, 1970

94   G. Easterbrook, 1997

95   L. Bickel, p. 353

96   WFP nomination criteria

97   K. Kautzky, 2019

Backmatter

98   J. Carter, 2010.

99   "Dr. Norman Borlaug: Stars," 1997.
           youtu.be/nACAyqoWScY?list=PL93EA3145F56ADD86
           Texas A& M "Dr. Norman Borlaug: Stars." *AgriLife Video*.

About the Author

Peggy Thomas is the author of more than twenty award-winning nonfiction books for children including *Lincoln Clears a Path: Abraham Lincoln's Agricultural Legacy*, illustrated by Stacy Innerst, and *Full of Beans: Henry Ford Grows a Car*, illustrated by Edwin Fotheringham, which earned the AFBFA 2020 Book of the Year Award. From her home in Middleport, NY, Peggy frequently speaks at schools, libraries, and conferences, promoting food security through her writing and in her own garden. A portion of all proceeds from this book will help support her local food pantry.

Learn more at
www.peggythomaswrites.com